הגדת התפוצות
The DIASPORA HAGGADAH
The Artistic and Transliterated
Haggadah of Passover
English Edition

REMOVE THE LEAVEN ביעור חמץ

אור לארבעה עשר בניסן, מיד לאחר תפילת ערבית, בודקים את החמץ לאור הנר, בכל מקום בבית, בעבודה ובמכונית. (אם חל בשבת בודקים אור לשלושה-עשר). ייסול ידיו ויברך:

On the night preceding Passover Eve it is customary to search for bread or leaven throughout the house.

בָּרוּךְ אַתָּה יְיָ אֱלֹהֵינוּ מֶלֶךְ הָעוֹלָם אֲשֶׁר קִדְּשָׁנוּ בְּמִצְוֹתָיו וְצִוָּנוּ עַל בִּעוּר חָמֵץ

Blessed are you, Lord our God, King of the Universe, who made us holy with His commandments, and commanded us to remove the leaven.

Baruch ata Adonay, Eloheyno melech ha'olam, asher kidshanu bemitzvotav ve'tzivanu al beur chametz.

After the leaven has been gathered and wrapped securely, the following is to be said: אחר הבדיקה יאמר:

כָּל חֲמִירָא וַחֲמִיעָא דְּאִכָּא בִרְשׁוּתִי דְּלָא חֲמִתֵּהּ וּדְלָא בְעַרְתֵּהּ
וּדְלָא יְדַעְנָא לֵהּ לִבָּטֵיל וְלֶהֱוֵי הֶפְקֵר כְּעַפְרָא דְאַרְעָא

Any leaven that may still be in the house, which I have not seen or have not removed, shall be as if it does not exist and as the dust of the earth.

Kol chamira va'chamia de'ika virshuti dela chamite u'dela viarteh u'dela yad'ana le livtil ve'lehevei hefker ke'afra de'araa.

ערב פסח שחרית, לפני צאתו לעבודה, עד השעה עשר בקירוב, שורף את החמץ ומבטלו בלבו. ואומר:

On the eve of Passover, about ten o'clock in the morning, at the burning of the leaven, the following is recited.

כָּל חֲמִירָא וַחֲמִיעָא דְּאִכָּא בִרְשׁוּתִי דַּחֲמִתֵּהּ וּדְלָא חֲמִתֵּהּ דְּבְעַרְתֵּהּ
וּדְלָא בְעַרְתֵּהּ לִבָּטֵיל וְלֶהֱוֵי הֶפְקֵר כְּעַפְרָא דְאַרְעָא

Any leaven that may still be in the house, which I have or have not seen, which I have or have not removed, shall be as if it does not exist and as the dust of the earth.

Kol chamira va'chamia de'ika virshuti dachamite u'dela chamite, de'viarteh udela viarteh livtil ve'lehevei hefker ke'afra de'araa.

MIXING OF FOODS עירוב תבשילין

בחו"ל, אם חל ערב פסח ביום רביעי, עושים עירוב תבשילין. נוטל מצה ותבשיל ומברך:

When Passover falls on a Friday, in order that it may be permissible to cook on that day for Saturday (one is permitted to cook on a holiday for that day alone), the head of the household must perform the ritual of "Eruv Tavshilin" before the festival. This consists of taking some matzah and some other food, such as fish or meat, putting them on a plate, lifting it, and then reciting the following prayers:

בָּרוּךְ אַתָּה יְיָ אֱלֹהֵינוּ מֶלֶךְ הָעוֹלָם אֲשֶׁר קִדְּשָׁנוּ בְּמִצְוֹתָיו וְצִוָּנוּ עַל מִצְוַת עֵרוּב

Blessed are you, Lord our God, King of the Universe, who made us holy with His commandments, and commanded us concerning the Eruv.

Baruch ata Adonay, Eloheynu melech ha'olam, asher kidshanu bemitzvotav ve'tzivanu al mitzvat eruv.

בַּהֲדֵין עֵרוּבָא יְהֵא שָׁרֵא לָנָא לְמֵפָא וּלְבַשָּׁלָא וּלְאַטְמָנָא וּלְאַדְלָקָא
שְׁרָגָא וּלְמֶעְבַּד כָּל צָרְכָּנָא מִיּוֹמָא טָבָא לְשַׁבְּתָא לָנוּ וּלְכָל הַדָּרִים בָּעִיר הַזֹּאת

With this Eruv, it shall be permissible for us to bake, cook, and to keep the food warm, to light the candles, and to prepare all necessary things on the festival for the Shabbat. This shall be permitted to us and to all Jews who live in this city.

Bahadein eruva yehe share lana lemefe u'levashla u'leatmana u'leadlaka sheraga u'leme'bad kol tzorkana mi'yoma tava le'shabta lanu u'lechol ha'darim ba'ir ha'zot.

THE SETTING OF THE SEDER TABLE

Arranged in a circle on the Seder plate, which is placed in the center of the table, are several types of food, each representing an historic aspect of Passover. (The precise foods differ according to the traditions of each Jewish ethnic group.)

The Shank Bone:
A leg joint (lamb or chicken) represents the Lord's "outstretched arm" that brought the Israelites out of bondage in Egypt. The roasted leg joint symbolizes the original Passover sacrifice. It will not be eaten at the Seder as we are forbidden to eat "the Passover meat offering." It may, however, be eaten the next day.

The Egg:
A boiled or roasted egg, traditionally eaten when one is in mourning, commemorates the destruction of the Holy Temple. As it is said: "I shall hold Jerusalem above my greatest joys."

Karpas:
Karpas can be one of several vegetables: parsley, celery, radish or potato. The "Karpas" is dipped into salt water and eaten, recalling the tears shed by our ancestors in slavery.

Marror (bitter herbs):
To recall that the "Egyptians made our forefathers' lives bitter," lettuce is eaten after dipping it into charoset, a mixture of groundnuts, fruits, spices and wine. Not too much charoset is eaten so as not to sweeten the taste excessively.

Charoset:
Charoset is symbolic of the mortar with which our ancestors made bricks for the Egyptians. Red wine, which thins the charoset mixture, recalls the blood of Israelite newborn males who were killed by Pharoah's decree.

Chazeret:
This was originally lettuce, i.e., bitter herbs (maror). However today, Seder plates include "cherraine" (horseradish), which is also (mistakenly) called chazeret. This Seder custom originated with Eastern European Jews who ate the horseradish with lettuce and Matzah in a "Korech" (sandwich) to enhance the bitter taste and hence, the symbolic bitterness.

עריכת שלחן הסדר

במרכז השולחן עומדת ה"קערה", ובה מסדרים מאכלים שונים שבהם מקיימים את מצוות ליל הסדר, ושמסמלים מאורעות היסטוריים הקשורים בפסח, בשעבוד במצרים ובגאולה. תכולת ה"קערה" וסדר מאכלים שבה תלויים במנהג ושונים מעט מעדה לעדה.

הזרוע:
לוקחים זרוע (שוק) של כבש או עוף - זכר ל"זרוע נטויה" שבה גאל הקב"ה את ישראל ממצרים, וצולים אותה באש- זכר לקרבן פסח שהיה "צלי-אש". את הזרוע אין אוכלים אלא למחרת ביום, בגלל המנהג שלא לאכול בשר צלוי בליל הסדר - "שמא יאמרו בשר (קרבן) פסח הוא".

הביצה:
שולקים אותה או צולים אותה, ונוהגים לאכלה כזכר לחרבן המקדש, שהביצה היא מאכל אבלים, לקיים "אעלה את ירושלים על ראש שמחתי".

המרור:
"על שום שמררו המצרים את חיי אבותינו במצרים". מבין סוגי הירק הכשרים לצרך מצוות אכילת מרור נהוג לאכל את החזרת, היא החסה. את המרור טובלים בחרוסת כדי להפיג מעט את המרירות שבו, אך אין מרבים בחרוסת שלא להמתיק את המרור לגמרי.

החרסת:
מרסקים ומערבבים ביחד תמרים ואגוזים, ויש המוסיפים עוד מינים כתפוחים, אגסים, שקדים או תבלינים שונים. את העיסה המתקבלת - זכר לטיט שבו העבידו המצרים את אבותינו - מדללים מעט ביין אדום - זכר לדם ילדי ישראל ששפך פרעה, לפי האגדה.

הכרפס:
הוא מין ירק, אך במקומו נוהגים לאכל סוגים שונים של ירק, כגון פטרוסיליה, סלרי, צנון או תפוחי-אדמה. את ה"כרפס" טובלים במי מלח.

החזרת:
היא, כאמור, חסה - כלומר: מרור. ואמנם יש אגדות שבהן מצוירת ה"קערה", ובה במקום "חזרת", כתוב פעם שניה "מרור". בימינו קוראים בטעות חזרת לשרש המר הקרוי בלעז "כריין". מקור הטעות הוא במנהג (של יהודי מזרח אירופה) להוסיף מן השרש הזה לחסה הנאכלת עם המצה (כורך) לשם הגברת המרירות.

KADESH
RECITING THE KIDDUSH

URECHATZ
WASHING THE HANDS

KARPAS
DIPPING VEGETABLES IN SALT WATER

YACHATZ
BREAKING THE MIDDLE MATZAH AND HIDING A HALF OF IT FOR AFIKOMAN

MAGGID
RECITING THE PASSOVER STORY

RACHTZA
WASHING THE HANDS BEFORE THE MEAL

MOTZI MATZA
PARTAKING OF THE MATZAH

MAROR
EATING THE BITTER HERB

KORECH
EATING THE BITTER HERB AND MATZAH TOGETHER

SHULCHAN ORECH
SERVING THE FESTIVAL MEAL

TZAFUN
PARTAKING OF THE AFIKOMAN

BARECH
SAYING THE GRACE AFTER MEAL

HALELL
RECITING OF THE "HALLEL"

NIRTZAH
THE SEDER WAS ACCEPTED

The first cup of wine is filled, and held in the right hand. Then the blessing is recited.

מוזגים כוס ראשון. נוטלו ביד ימינו ומקדש
הנני מוכן ומזומן לקיים מצוות כוס ראשון של ארבע כוסות לשם ייחוד
קודשא בריך הוא שכינתיה, על ידי ההוא טמיר ונעלם בשם כל ישראל.

KADESH
RECITE THE KIDDUSH

On the eve of Sabbath begin here:　　　　　　　　　בליל שבת מתחילין כאן:

וַיְהִי עֶרֶב וַיְהִי בֹקֶר
יוֹם הַשִּׁשִּׁי וַיְכֻלּוּ הַשָּׁמַיִם וְהָאָרֶץ וְכָל צְבָאָם: וַיְכַל אֱלֹהִים
בַּיּוֹם הַשְּׁבִיעִי מְלַאכְתּוֹ אֲשֶׁר עָשָׂה, וַיִּשְׁבֹּת בַּיּוֹם הַשְּׁבִיעִי מִכָּל
מְלַאכְתּוֹ אֲשֶׁר עָשָׂה, וַיְבָרֶךְ אֱלֹהִים אֶת יוֹם הַשְּׁבִיעִי וַיְקַדֵּשׁ אֹתוֹ.
כִּי בוֹ שָׁבַת מִכָּל מְלַאכְתּוֹ, אֲשֶׁר בָּרָא אֱלֹהִים לַעֲשׂוֹת.

And it was evening and it was morning

IT was the sixth day that the heaven and earth were completed in all their array. On the seventh day God completed all the work He had made, and He rested on the seventh day from all His work which He had made. Then God blessed the seventh day and made it holy for on it He rested from all His work which He had created and made.

Yom Ha'shishi va'yechulu hashamayim veha'aretz ve'chol tzevaam: va'yechal Elohim bayom ha'shevii melachto asher asa, va'yishbot bayom ha'shevii mikol melachto asher asa, va'yevarech Elohim et yom ha'shevii va'yekadesh oto ki vo shavat mikol melachto asher bara Elohim la'asot.

On on weekday begin here
(On Sabbath add the words in parentheses)

בשאר ימות השבוע מתחילין כאן

בָּרוּךְ אַתָּה, יְיָ אֱלֹהֵינוּ מֶלֶךְ הָעוֹלָם בּוֹרֵא פְּרִי הַגָּפֶן:

בָּרוּךְ אַתָּה יְיָ אֱלֹהֵינוּ מֶלֶךְ הָעוֹלָם אֲשֶׁר בָּחַר בָּנוּ מִכָּל עָם, וְרוֹמְמָנוּ מִכָּל לָשׁוֹן, וְקִדְּשָׁנוּ בְּמִצְוֹתָיו. וַתִּתֶּן לָנוּ יְיָ אֱלֹהֵינוּ בְּאַהֲבָה (לשבת: שַׁבָּתוֹת לִמְנוּחָה וּ) מוֹעֲדִים לְשִׂמְחָה, חַגִּים וּזְמַנִּים לְשָׂשׂוֹן, (לשבת אֶת יוֹם הַשַּׁבָּת הַזֶּה וְ) אֶת יוֹם חַג הַמַּצּוֹת הַזֶּה זְמַן חֵרוּתֵנוּ (לשבת בְּאַהֲבָה) מִקְרָא קֹדֶשׁ זֵכֶר לִיצִיאַת מִצְרָיִם כִּי בָנוּ בָחַרְתָּ וְאוֹתָנוּ קִדַּשְׁתָּ מִכָּל הָעַמִּים (לשבת וְשַׁבָּת) וּמוֹעֲדֵי קָדְשֶׁךָ (לשבת בְּאַהֲבָה וּבְרָצוֹן) בְּשִׂמְחָה וּבְשָׂשׂוֹן הִנְחַלְתָּנוּ, בָּרוּךְ אַתָּה יְיָ מְקַדֵּשׁ (לשבת הַשַּׁבָּת וְ) יִשְׂרָאֵל וְהַזְּמַנִּים:

Baruch ata Adonay Eloheynu melech ha'olam bore peri ha'gafen

Baruch ata Adonay Eloheynu melech ha'olam asher bachar banu mikol am veromemanu mikol lashon vekidshanu bemitzvotav. Vatiten lanu Adonay Eloheynu be'ahava (li'shabat: shabatot limenucha u) moadim lesimcha chagim uzemanim lesason (le'shabat: et yom hashabat haze ve) et yom chag hamatzot haze, zeman cherutenu (le'shabat: be'ahava) mikra kodesh zecher lytziat Mitzraim ki vanu bacharta ve'otanu kidashta mikol ha'amim (le'shabat: ve'shabat) u'moadei kodshecha (le'shabat: be'ahava uveratzon) besimcha u've'sason hinchaltanu. Baruch ata Adonay mekadesh (le'shabat: hashabat ve) Israel vehazemanim.

Blessed are you, Lord our God, King of the Universe, who created the fruit of the vine. Blessed are you, Lord our God, King of the Universe, who has chosen us from all peoples and singled us out among all other nations by sanctifying us with your commandments. You have lovingly given us, Lord our God, (the Sabbaths for rest and) times for gladness, festivals and set seasons for rejoicing (this Sabbath day and) this day of the Feast of unleavened Bread, the season of our Liberation (in Love) and a holy assembly as a memorial of the exodus from Egypt; for you have chosen us and sanctified us above all peoples, you have given us the heritage (in love and favour) in joy and gladness of your holy (Sabbath and) festivals. Blessed are you, O Lord, who hallows (the Sabbath and) Israel and the festive seasons.

במוצאי שבת מוסיפים ברכה זו לפני ברכת "שהחיינו".

בָּרוּךְ

אַתָּה יְיָ אֱלֹהֵינוּ מֶלֶךְ הָעוֹלָם בּוֹרֵא מְאוֹרֵי הָאֵשׁ

בָּרוּךְ אַתָּה יְיָ אֱלֹהֵינוּ מֶלֶךְ הָעוֹלָם הַמַּבְדִּיל בֵּין קֹדֶשׁ לְחֹל, בֵּין אוֹר לְחֹשֶׁךְ, בֵּין יִשְׂרָאֵל לָעַמִּים, בֵּין יוֹם הַשְּׁבִיעִי לְשֵׁשֶׁת יְמֵי הַמַּעֲשֶׂה, בֵּין קְדֻשַּׁת שַׁבָּת לִקְדֻשַּׁת יוֹם טוֹב הִבְדַּלְתָּ, וְאֶת יוֹם הַשְּׁבִיעִי מִשֵּׁשֶׁת יְמֵי הַמַּעֲשֶׂה קִדָּשְׁתָּ. הִבְדַּלְתָּ וְקִדַּשְׁתָּ אֶת עַמְּךָ יִשְׂרָאֵל בִּקְדֻשָּׁתֶךָ. בָּרוּךְ אַתָּה יְיָ הַמַּבְדִּיל בֵּין קֹדֶשׁ לְקֹדֶשׁ.

On Saturday night the following is added:

Blessed are you, Lord our God, King of the Universe, who created the light of the fire. Blessed are you, Lord our God, King of the Universe, who makes a distinction between sacred and profane, light and darkness, Israel and the other peoples, the seventh day and the six working days. You have made a distinction between the holiness of the Sabbath and the sanctity of the festival, and have hallowed the seventh day above the six working days; you have distinguished and hallowed your people Israel by our holiness. Blessed are you, Lord, who makes a distinction between holy and holy.

Baruch ata Adonay Eloheynu melech ha'olam bore me'orey ha'esh
Baruch ata Adonay Eloheynu melech ha'olam hamavdil bein kodesh le'chol, bein or le'choshech, bein Israel la'amim, bein yom hashevii lesheshet yemey hama'ase. Bein kedushat shabat li'kedushat yom tov hivdalta, ve'et yom hashevii misheshet yemey hama'ase kidashta. Hivdalta vekidashta et amcha Israel bikedushatecha. Baruch ata Adonay hamavdil bein kodesh le'kodesh.

בָּרוּךְ אַתָּה

יְיָ אֱלֹהֵינוּ מֶלֶךְ הָעוֹלָם
שֶׁהֶחֱיָנוּ וְקִיְּמָנוּ וְהִגִּיעָנוּ לַזְּמַן הַזֶּה.

שותים כוס ראשונה בהסבת שמאל
Drink the first cup of wine.

Baruch ata Adonay Eloheinu melech
ha'olam shehecheyanu ve'kymanu
ve'higianu lazeman ha'ze.

מביאים לבעל הבית מים
נוטל ידיו ואינו מברך

נוטל מהכרפס פחות מכזית
טובלו במי-מלח ומברך:

בָּרוּךְ אַתָּה יְיָ אֱלֹהֵינוּ מֶלֶךְ הָעוֹלָם
בּוֹרֵא פְּרִי הָאֲדָמָה.

Baruch ata Adonay Eloheinu melech
ha'olam, bore peri ha'adama.

מחלק את המצה האמצעית
לשני חלקים, מצפין את החלק
הגדול כאפיקומן ומחזיר
החלק הקטן למקומו

מגביה את הקערה, מראה על המצה
הפרוסה שבין שתי השלמות ואומר:
הנני מוכן ומזומן לקיים המצווה
לספר ביציאת מצרים לשם ייחוד
קודשא בריך הוא ושכינתיה, על ידי
ההוא טמיר ונעלם בשם כל ישראל.

Blessed are you, Lord our God, King of the Universe, who has kept us alive and preserved us and enabled us to reach this happy season.

URECHATZ
Washing the Hands. The gathering wash their hands, but do not recite the customary blessing.

KARPAS
The leader takes the Karpas (i.e., parsley, radishes, celery or potato) and dips it in salt water or vinegar and gives a small piece to each participant. Before eating it, the following blessing is recited:

Blessed are you, Lord our God, King of the Universe, who creates the fruit of the earth.

YACHATZ
Dividing the Middle Matzah. The Leader breaks the middle Matzah, leaving one half between the two whole ones and setting aside the other half as the Afikoman.

MAGGID
Narration of the story of the Exodus begins. The Matzot are uncovered, the ceremonial dish is raised and the leader recites the following:

הָא לַחְמָא עַנְיָא דִּי אֲכָלוּ אַבְהָתָנָא בְּאַרְעָא דְמִצְרָיִם. כָּל דִּכְפִין יֵיתֵי וְיֵכֹל. כָּל דִּצְרִיךְ יֵיתֵי וְיִפְסַח. הָשַׁתָּא הָכָא. לְשָׁנָה הַבָּאָה בְּאַרְעָא דְיִשְׂרָאֵל. הָשַׁתָּא עַבְדֵי. לְשָׁנָה הַבָּאָה בְּנֵי חוֹרִין:

This is the bread of affliction which our fathers ate in the land of Egypt. Let those who are hungry come in and partake. Let all who are in need come and celebrate the Passover. Now we are here but next year may we be in the land of Israel. Now we are slaves but in the year to come may we be free men.

Ha lachma anya, di achalu avhatana be'ara de'Mitzrayim. Kol dichfin yeytei ve'yechol.
Kol ditzrich yeytei ve'yifsach.
Ha'shata hacha. Le'shana haba'a be'araa de'Israel.
Ha'shata avdei.
Le'shana haba'a benei chorin.

The second cup of wine is filled, the plate is put down, and the Matzah is covered. The youngest at the table asks the Four Questions:

מוזגים כוס שני, מסלקים את הקערה ומכסים את המצות, כאן הבן שואל:

How is this night different from any other night?
On any other night we eat levened and unleavened bread, why on this night only unleavened bread?
On any other night we eat any kind of herbs, why on this night only bitter herbs?
On any other night we do not dip our herbs into anything even once, why on this night do we do it twice? On any other night we eat either sitting upright or reclining, why on this night do we all recline?

שֶׁבְּכָל הַלֵּילוֹת אָנוּ אוֹכְלִין חָמֵץ וּמַצָּה הַלַּיְלָה הַזֶּה כֻּלּוֹ מַצָּה

שֶׁבְּכָל הַלֵּילוֹת אָנוּ אוֹכְלִין שְׁאָר יְרָקוֹת הַלַּיְלָה הַזֶּה (כֻּלּוֹ) מָרוֹר

שֶׁבְּכָל הַלֵּילוֹת אֵין אָנוּ מַטְבִּילִין אֲפִילוּ פַּעַם אֶחָת הַלַּיְלָה הַזֶּה שְׁתֵּי פְעָמִים

שֶׁבְּכָל הַלֵּילוֹת אָנוּ אוֹכְלִין בֵּין יוֹשְׁבִין וּבֵין מְסֻבִּין הַלַּיְלָה הַזֶּה כֻּלָּנוּ מְסֻבִּין

Ma nishtana ha'layla haze mikol ha'leylot? Shebechol ha'leylot anu ochlin chametz umatzah, ha'layla haze kulo matzah. Shebechol ha'leylot anu ochlin shear yerakot, halayla haze (kulo) marror. Shebechol ha'leylot ein anu matbilin afilu paam achat, ha'layla haze, shetei pe'amim. Shebechol ha'leylot anu ochlin bein yoshvin u'vein mesubin, ha'layla haze kulanu mesubin.

Uncover the Matzot and begin the reply:

עֲבָדִים הָיִינוּ לְפַרְעֹה בְּמִצְרַיִם. וַיּוֹצִיאֵנוּ יְיָ אֱלֹהֵינוּ מִשָּׁם בְּיָד חֲזָקָה וּבִזְרֹעַ נְטוּיָה. וְאִלּוּ לֹא הוֹצִיא הַקָּדוֹשׁ בָּרוּךְ הוּא אֶת אֲבוֹתֵינוּ מִמִּצְרַיִם הֲרֵי אָנוּ וּבָנֵינוּ וּבְנֵי בָנֵינוּ מְשֻׁעְבָּדִים הָיִינוּ לְפַרְעֹה בְּמִצְרָיִם. וַאֲפִילוּ כֻּלָּנוּ חֲכָמִים, כֻּלָּנוּ נְבוֹנִים, כֻּלָּנוּ זְקֵנִים, כֻּלָּנוּ יוֹדְעִים אֶת הַתּוֹרָה, מִצְוָה עָלֵינוּ לְסַפֵּר בִּיצִיאַת מִצְרָיִם וְכָל הַמַּרְבֶּה לְסַפֵּר בִּיצִיאַת מִצְרַיִם הֲרֵי זֶה מְשֻׁבָּח.

Slaves were we to Pharoah in Egypt and the Lord our God brought us out from there with a mighty hand and outstretched arm. If the Holy One, Blessed be He, had not brought our fathers out of Egypt, then we and our children and our children's children would still be enslaved to Pharoah in Egypt. Therefore, if all of us were wise, all mature, all versed in the Torah, it would still be our duty to tell the story of the Liberation from Egypt. The more one dwells upon the details of the Exodus, the more he is praised.

Avadim hayinu le'Par'o be'Mitzraim. va'yotzienu Adonay Eloheinu misham beyad chazaka u'vi'zeroa netuya. ve'ilu lo hotzi ha'kadosh baruch hu et avoteinu mi'Mitzraim harei anu u'vaneinu uvnei vaneinu meshuabadim hayinu le'Par'o be'Mitzraim, va'afilu kulanu chachamim, kulanu nevonim, kulanu yod'im et ha'tora, mitzva aleinu le'saper bitziat mitzraim. ve'chol hamarbe lesaper bitziat mitzraim harey ze meshubach.

מַעֲשֶׂה בְּרַבִּי אֱלִיעֶזֶר וְרַבִּי יְהוֹשֻׁעַ וְרַבִּי אֶלְעָזָר בֶּן עֲזַרְיָה וְרַבִּי עֲקִיבָא וְרַבִּי טַרְפוֹן שֶׁהָיוּ מְסֻבִּין בִּבְנֵי בְרַק, וְהָיוּ מְסַפְּרִים בִּיצִיאַת מִצְרַיִם כָּל אוֹתוֹ הַלַּיְלָה, עַד שֶׁבָּאוּ תַלְמִידֵיהֶם וְאָמְרוּ לָהֶם רַבּוֹתֵינוּ, הִגִּיעַ זְמַן קְרִיאַת שְׁמַע שֶׁל שַׁחֲרִית:

It once happened that Rabbi Eliezer, Rabbi Joshua, Rabbi Eleazar ben Azariah, Rabbi Akiba, and Rabbi Tarphon gathered together in Bene Berak and they discussed the Exodus throughout the night until their disciples came and said to them: "Our teachers, it is time to recite the morning Shema."

Ma'ase be'rabi Eliezer ve'rabi Yehoshua ve'rabi Elazar ben Azaria ve'rabi Akiva ve'rabi Tarphon she'hayu mesubin bivnei brak, ve'hayu mesaprim bytzi'at Mitzraim kol oto ha'layla, ad shebau talmideihem ve'amru lahem: Raboteinu, higia zeman keriat shema shel shacharit.

אָמַר רַבִּי אֶלְעָזָר בֶּן עֲזַרְיָה: הֲרֵי אֲנִי כְּבֶן שִׁבְעִים שָׁנָה, וְלֹא זָכִיתִי שֶׁתֵּאָמֵר יְצִיאַת מִצְרַיִם בַּלֵּילוֹת, עַד שֶׁדְּרָשָׁהּ בֶּן זוֹמָא. שֶׁנֶּאֱמַר לְמַעַן תִּזְכֹּר אֶת יוֹם צֵאתְךָ מֵאֶרֶץ מִצְרַיִם כֹּל יְמֵי חַיֶּיךָ: יְמֵי חַיֶּיךָ הַיָּמִים, כֹּל יְמֵי חַיֶּיךָ הַלֵּילוֹת, וַחֲכָמִים אוֹמְרִים יְמֵי חַיֶּיךָ הָעוֹלָם הַזֶּה. כֹּל יְמֵי חַיֶּיךָ לְהָבִיא לִימוֹת הַמָּשִׁיחַ:

Rabbi Eleazar ben Azariah said: I am a man of seventy and yet I did not understand why the story of the departure from Egypt should be related at night until Ben Zoma explained: "It is said' you will remember the day when you came out of the land of Egypt all the days of your life' (Deut. 16:3). 'The days of your life' would have meant the days only, but 'all the days of your life' includes the nights also." The Sages further maintain that "The days of your life" refers to this world, while "All the days of your life" is taken to include the days of the Messiah.

Amar Rabi Elazar ben Azaria: harei ani keven shiv'im shana, ve'lo zachiti shete'amer yetziat Mitzrayim baleilot, ad shederasha ben Zoma. Sheneemar: lema'an tizkor et yom tzetcha me'eretz Mitzrayim kol yemei chayecha." "yemei chayecha," hayamim: "kol yemei chayecha," haleylot: Va'chachamim omrim: yemei chayecha," ha'olam ha'ze;" Kol yemei chayecha," le'havi lymot hamashiach.

בָּרוּךְ הַמָּקוֹם בָּרוּךְ הוּא. בָּרוּךְ שֶׁנָּתַן תּוֹרָה לְעַמּוֹ יִשְׂרָאֵל בָּרוּךְ הוּא:

Blessed be God, Blessed be He. Blessed be the One who gave the Torah to His people Israel, Blessed be He. The Torah speaks of four kinds of children, the wise, the wicked, the simple and the one who is too young to ask.

Baruch ha'makom baruch hu. Baruch shenatan tora le'amo Israel Baruch hu.
Keneged arba'a banim dibra tora. Echad chacham, ve'echad rasha, ve'echad tam, ve'echad she'eyno yodea lish'ol:

כְּנֶגֶד אַרְבָּעָה בָנִים דִּבְּרָה תוֹרָה. אֶחָד חָכָם, וְאֶחָד רָשָׁע, וְאֶחָד תָּם, וְאֶחָד שֶׁאֵינוֹ יוֹדֵעַ לִשְׁאוֹל:

מַה הוּא אוֹמֵר. מָה הָעֵדוֹת וְהַחֻקִּים וְהַמִּשְׁפָּטִים אֲשֶׁר צִוָּה יְיָ אֱלֹהֵינוּ אֶתְכֶם. וְאַף אַתָּה אֱמֹר לוֹ כְּהִלְכוֹת הַפֶּסַח: אֵין מַפְטִירִין אַחַר הַפֶּסַח אֲפִיקוֹמָן.

What does the wise son ask? What mean the testimonies, the statutes, and the ordinances, "which the Lord our God commanded you" (Deut. 6:20)? It is then your duty to tell him all the laws of the Passover down to the last detail of the Afikoman.

What does the wicked son say? "What does this service mean to you?" (Ex. 2:26). Since he says "To you" and not "to himself", he excludes himself and thus denies God. Refute his arguments and tell him: "This is done because of that which the Lord did for me when I came out of Egypt." "For me" not for him, implying that if he had been there, he would not have been redeemed.

Chacham ma hu omer: ma ha'edot ve'ha'chukim ve'ha'mishpatim asher tziva adonay eloheynu etchem ve'af ata emor lokehilchot ha'pesach: ein maftirin achar ha'pesach afikoman.

Rasha ma hu omer: ma ha'avoda ha'zot lachem, lachem velo lo. u'lefi shehotzi et atzmo min hakelal kafar be'ikar. ve'af ata hakhee et shinav ve'emor lo: ba'avur ze asa adonay li betzeti mi'Mitzrayim: li ve'lo lo. ilu haya sham lo haya nigal.

מַה הוּא אוֹמֵר. מָה הָעֲבוֹדָה הַזֹּאת לָכֶם. לָכֶם וְלֹא לוֹ. וּלְפִי שֶׁהוֹצִיא אֶת עַצְמוֹ מִן הַכְּלָל כָּפַר בְּעִקָּר. וְאַף אַתָּה הַקְהֵה אֶת שִׁנָּיו וֶאֱמֹר לוֹ. בַּעֲבוּר זֶה עָשָׂה יְיָ לִי בְּצֵאתִי מִמִּצְרָיִם: לִי וְלֹא לוֹ. אִלּוּ הָיָה שָׁם לֹא הָיָה נִגְאָל.

תָּם מַה הוּא אוֹמֵר. מַה זֹּאת. וְאָמַרְתָּ אֵלָיו בְּחֹזֶק יָד הוֹצִיאָנוּ יְיָ מִמִּצְרַיִם מִבֵּית עֲבָדִים.

What does the simple son ask? "What is this?" (Ex. 13:14). You shall say to him: "By strength of his hand, the Lord brought us out of Egypt, from the house of bondage."

Tam ma hu omer: ma zot? Ve'amarta elav: be'chozek yad hotzianu Adonay mi'Mitzrayim mibeit avadim.

To the son who is too young to ask, you shall tell him: it is said (Ex. 13:8), "On that day you shall tell your son, 'This commemorates what the Lord did for me when I came out of Egypt.'"

Veshe'eyno yodea lish'ol at petach lo. She'ne'emar: ve'higadeta le'vincha ba'yom ha'hu le'emor: ba'avur ze asa Adonay li be'tzeti mi'Mitzrayim.

יָכוֹל מֵרֹאשׁ חֹדֶשׁ, תַּלְמוּד לוֹמַר בַּיּוֹם הַהוּא. אִי בַּיּוֹם הַהוּא, יָכוֹל מִבְּעוֹד יוֹם. תַּלְמוּד לוֹמַר בַּעֲבוּר זֶה. בַּעֲבוּר זֶה לֹא אָמַרְתִּי, אֶלָּא בְּשָׁעָה שֶׁיֵּשׁ מַצָּה וּמָרוֹר מֻנָּחִים לְפָנֶיךָ:

It could be said that the Passover story could be related at the beginning of the month. The text, however, stresses "On that day." If it is to be "on that day," one might think that the story should begin in the daytime. The text says "because of that," referring to the time when "unleavened bread and bitter herbs are placed before you."

Yachol me'rosh chodesh? Talmud lomar: ba'yom ha'hu. I ba'yom ha'hu, yachol mibeod yom? Talmud lomar: ba'avur ze. "Ba'avur ze" lo amarti ela be'shaa sheyesh matza u'maror munachim lefanecha.

מִתְּחִלָּה עוֹבְדֵי עֲבוֹדָה זָרָה הָיוּ אֲבוֹתֵינוּ וְעַכְשָׁיו קֵרְבָנוּ הַמָּקוֹם לַעֲבוֹדָתוֹ. שֶׁנֶּאֱמַר: וַיֹּאמֶר יְהוֹשֻׁעַ אֶל כָּל הָעָם: כֹּה אָמַר יְיָ אֱלֹהֵי יִשְׂרָאֵל: בְּעֵבֶר הַנָּהָר יָשְׁבוּ אֲבוֹתֵיכֶם מֵעוֹלָם, תֶּרַח אֲבִי אַבְרָהָם וַאֲבִי נָחוֹר, וַיַּעַבְדוּ אֱלֹהִים אֲחֵרִים: וָאֶקַּח אֶת אֲבִיכֶם אֶת אַבְרָהָם מֵעֵבֶר הַנָּהָר, וָאוֹלֵךְ אוֹתוֹ בְּכָל אֶרֶץ כְּנָעַן. וָאַרְבֶּה אֶת זַרְעוֹ, וָאֶתֵּן לוֹ אֶת יִצְחָק, וָאֶתֵּן לְיִצְחָק אֶת יַעֲקֹב וְאֶת עֵשָׂו, וָאֶתֵּן לְעֵשָׂו אֶת הַר שֵׂעִיר לָרֶשֶׁת אוֹתוֹ. וְיַעֲקֹב וּבָנָיו יָרְדוּ מִצְרָיִם:

In the beginning our ancestors worshipped idols but now the Almighty has drawn us to His service, as it is said (Josh.,24): "And Joshua said to all the people, 'This is the word of the Lord, the God of Israel: Long ago, Terah, father of Abraham and the father of Nahor, lived beyond the River and they served other gods. But I took your father Abraham from beyond the River and led him throughout the land of Canaan and multiplied his seed giving him Isaac. Unto Isaac I gave Jacob and Esau. I gave Esau the inheritance of Mount Seir and Jacob and his sons went down to Egypt.'"

Mitechila ovdei avoda zara hayu avoteinu, ve'achshav kervanu ha'Makom la'avodato, shene'emar: va'yomer yehoshua el kol ha'am: ko amar Adonay Elohey Israel: be'ever hanahar yashvu avoteichem me'olam, Terach avi Avraham va' avi Nachor, va'yaavdu elohim acherim. Va'ekach et avichem et Avraham me'ever ha'nahar va'olech oto bechol eretz Kenaan. Va'arbe et zaroo, va'eten lo et Yitzchak, va'eten le'Yitzchak et Yaakov ve'et Esav, va'eten le'Esav et har Seir lareshet oto Ve'Yaakov u'vanav yardu Mitzrayim.

שֶׁהַקָּדוֹשׁ בָּרוּךְ הוּא חִשַּׁב אֶת הַקֵּץ. לַעֲשׂוֹת כְּמָה שֶׁאָמַר לְאַבְרָהָם אָבִינוּ בִּבְרִית בֵּין הַבְּתָרִים. שֶׁנֶּאֱמַר: וַיֹּאמֶר לְאַבְרָם, יָדֹעַ תֵּדַע כִּי גֵר יִהְיֶה זַרְעֲךָ בְּאֶרֶץ לֹא לָהֶם, וַעֲבָדוּם וְעִנּוּ אוֹתָם אַרְבַּע מֵאוֹת שָׁנָה: וְגַם אֶת הַגּוֹי אֲשֶׁר יַעֲבֹדוּ דָּן אָנֹכִי, וְאַחֲרֵי כֵן יֵצְאוּ בִּרְכֻשׁ גָּדוֹל

Blessed be He who redeems His promise to Israel. Blessed be He! For the Holy One, blessed be He, was mindful of the end of the bondage so as to fulfill the promise made to Abraham our father at the Covenant of Sacrifice, as it is said (Gen.15:13-14): "And He said to Abram, 'Know for certain that your seed shall be strangers in a land that is not theirs; and they shall be enslaved and oppressed there for four hundred years. But also know I will judge that nation that they shall serve and thereafter they shall go forth with great substance."

Baruch shomer havtachato le Israel Baruch hu! She ha Kadosh Baruch Hu chishev et ha ketz. La asot kema she amar le' Avraham avinu bivrit bein ha'betarim. Shene'emar: va'yomer le' Avram, yadoa teda ki ger yihiye zar'acha be'eretz lo lahem, va'avadum ve'inu otam arba meot shana: ve'gam et ha'goy asher yaavodu dan anochi, ve'acharei chen yetz'u birechush gadol.

וְהִיא שֶׁעָמְדָה לַאֲבוֹתֵינוּ וְלָנוּ

שֶׁלֹּא אֶחָד בִּלְבָד עָמַד עָלֵינוּ לְכַלּוֹתֵנוּ. אֶלָּא שֶׁבְּכָל דּוֹר וָדוֹר עוֹמְדִים עָלֵינוּ לְכַלּוֹתֵנוּ. וְהַקָּדוֹשׁ בָּרוּךְ הוּא מַצִּילֵנוּ מִיָּדָם:

And this promise has been with our fathers and with us in every generation. Many have risen up against us to destroy us; in every generation. But the Holy One Blessed be He, delivers us from their hands.

Ve'hi she'amda, la'avoteinu ve'lanu, shelo echad bilvad amad aleinu lechaloteinu. Ela shebechol dor va'dor omdim aleinu lechaloteinu Ve'haKadosh Baruch Hu matzileinu miyadam.

מַה בִּקֵשׁ לָבָן הָאֲרַמִּי לַעֲשׂוֹת לְיַעֲקֹב אָבִינוּ. שֶׁפַּרְעֹה לֹא גָזַר אֶלָּא עַל הַזְּכָרִים וְלָבָן בִּקֵשׁ לַעֲקוֹר אֶת הַכֹּל. שֶׁנֶּאֱמַר: אֲרַמִּי אֹבֵד אָבִי. וַיֵּרֶד מִצְרַיְמָה וַיָּגָר שָׁם בִּמְתֵי מְעָט. וַיְהִי שָׁם לְגוֹי גָּדוֹל עָצוּם וָרָב:

Teach what Laban the Aramean wanted to do to our father Jacob. Whilst Pharaoh condemned to death only the newborn male children , Laban looked to destroy our whole people (Deut. 26:5).

Tze u'lemad ma bikesh Lavan ha'Arami laasot le'Yaacov avinu. She'Paro lo gazar ela al ha'zecharim ve'Lavan bikesh la'akor et ha'kol. She'neemar, Arami oved avi. Va'yered Mitzrayma, va'yagar sham bimtei me'at, va'yehi sham le'goy gadol atzum va'rav.

וַיֵּרֶד מִצְרַיְמָה

אָנוּס עַל פִּי הַדִּבּוּר: וַיָּגָר שָׁם מְלַמֵּד שֶׁלֹּא יָרַד יַעֲקֹב אָבִינוּ לְהִשְׁתַּקֵּעַ בְּמִצְרַיִם, אֶלָּא לָגוּר שָׁם. שֶׁנֶּאֱמַר: וַיֹּאמְרוּ אֶל פַּרְעֹה לָגוּר בָּאָרֶץ בָּאנוּ, כִּי אֵין מִרְעֶה לַצֹּאן אֲשֶׁר לַעֲבָדֶיךָ, כִּי כָבֵד הָרָעָב בְּאֶרֶץ כְּנָעַן. וְעַתָּה יֵשְׁבוּ נָא עֲבָדֶיךָ בְּאֶרֶץ גֹּשֶׁן:

בִּמְתֵי מְעָט, כְּמָה, שֶׁנֶּאֱמַר: בְּשִׁבְעִים נֶפֶשׁ יָרְדוּ אֲבוֹתֶיךָ מִצְרָיְמָה, וְעַתָּה שָׂמְךָ יְיָ אֱלֹהֶיךָ כְּכוֹכְבֵי הַשָּׁמַיִם לָרֹב:

וַיְהִי שָׁם לְגוֹי גָּדוֹל. מְלַמֵּד שֶׁהָיוּ יִשְׂרָאֵל מְצֻיָּנִים שָׁם: עָצוּם. כְּמָה שֶׁנֶּאֱמַר וּבְנֵי יִשְׂרָאֵל פָּרוּ וַיִּשְׁרְצוּ וַיִּרְבּוּ וַיַּעַצְמוּ בִּמְאֹד מְאֹד, וַתִּמָּלֵא הָאָרֶץ אוֹתָם:

וָרָב כְּמָה שֶׁנֶּאֱמַר: רְבָבָה כְּצֶמַח הַשָּׂדֶה נְתַתִּיךְ, וַתִּרְבִּי וַתִּגְדְּלִי, וַתָּבֹאִי בַּעֲדִי עֲדָיִים. שָׁדַיִם נָכֹנוּ, וּשְׂעָרֵךְ צִמֵּחַ, וְאַתְּ עֵרֹם וְעֶרְיָה: וָאֶעֱבֹר עָלַיִךְ וָאֶרְאֵךְ מִתְבּוֹסֶסֶת בְּדָמָיִךְ, וָאֹמַר לָךְ בְּדָמַיִךְ חֲיִי, וָאֹמַר לָךְ בְּדָמַיִךְ חֲיִי.

"Va'yered Mitzrayma" anus al pi ha'dibur. "Va'yagar sham melamed shelo yarad Yaacov avinu le'hishtakea be'Mitzrayim ela lagur sham. She'neemar: "va'yomru el Par'o: lagur ba'aretz banu, ki ein mir'e la'tzon asher la'avadecha, ki chaved ha'raav be'eretz Kenaan. Ve'ata yeshvu na avadecha be'eretz Goshen." "Bimetei me'at" kema shene'emar: "Beshiv'im nefesh yardu avoteinu Mitzrayma, ve'ata samcha Adonay Elohecha kechochvei ha'shamayim larov." "Va'yehi sham legoy gadol"-melamed shehayu Israel metzuyanim sham "Atzum" kema she'neemar: u'venei Israel paru va'yishretzu va'yirbu va'yaatzmu bim'od meod, va'timale ha'aretz otam." "Va'rav"-kema she'neemar: "revava ketzemach ha'sade netatich, va'tirbi va'tigdeli va'tavoi baadi adaayim. Shadayim nachonu, u'searech tzimeach, ve'at erom ve'erya: Va'eevor alayich va'er'ech mitboseset be'damayich va'omar lach, be'damayich chayi, be'damayich chayi."

"And he went down to Egypt few in number, and lived there until they became a great, powerful and numerous nation." "And he went down to Egypt," in obedience to the word of God. "And he sojourned there," this teaches that our father Jacob did not intend to settle in Egypt but meant to dwell there temporarily, as it is written (Gen. 47:4), "And they said to Pharoah: 'We have come to sojourn in the land, for there is no pasture for your servants, since the famine is so severe in the land of Canaan. So now, let your servants dwell in the land of Goshen.'" "Few in number," as it is said (Deut. 10:22), "With seventy persons your fathers went down to Egypt but now the Lord your God has made you as numerous as the stars in the sky." "And there they became a nation," teaching that the people of Israel distinguished themselves there. "Great and mighty," as it is said (Ex.1:7), "Now the children of Israel were fruitful and prolific: they multiplied and became great and strong and the land was filled with them." "And fertile," as it is said (Ex. 16:7), "I made you thrive like a plant (of the field), you grew into womanhood, your breasts became firm and your hair grew, but you were naked and vulnerable."

וַיָּרֵעוּ אֹתָנוּ הַמִּצְרִים. כְּמָה שֶׁנֶּאֱמַר: הָבָה נִתְחַכְּמָה לוֹ, פֶּן יִרְבֶּה וְהָיָה כִּי תִקְרֶאנָה מִלְחָמָה, וְנוֹסַף גַּם הוּא עַל שֹׂנְאֵינוּ וְנִלְחַם־בָּנוּ וְעָלָה מִן הָאָרֶץ.

וַיְעַנּוּנוּ. כְּמָה שֶׁנֶּאֱמַר: וַיָּשִׂימוּ עָלָיו שָׂרֵי מִסִּים לְמַעַן עַנֹּתוֹ בְּסִבְלֹתָם. וַיִּבֶן עָרֵי מִסְכְּנוֹת לְפַרְעֹה, אֶת־פִּתֹם וְאֶת־רַעַמְסֵס.

וַיִּתְּנוּ עָלֵינוּ עֲבֹדָה קָשָׁה. כְּמָה שֶׁנֶּאֱמַר: וַיַּעֲבִדוּ מִצְרַיִם אֶת־בְּנֵי יִשְׂרָאֵל בְּפָרֶךְ.

Vayareu otanu ha'Mitzrim va'ye'anunu, va'yitnu aleinu avoda kasha. "Va'yareu otanu ha'Mitzrim", kema shene'emar: "hava nitchakma lo, pen yirbe, ve'haya ki tikrena milchama ve'nosaf gam hu al son'einu, ve'nilcham banu, ve'ala min ha'aretz. "Va'ye'anunu," kema shene'emar: "Va'yasimu alav sarei misim le'maan anoto besivlotam. Va'yiven arei miskenot le'Par'o et Pitom, ve'et Ra'amses." "Va'yitnu aleinu avoda kasha," kema shene'emar: va'ya'avidu Mitzrayim et benei Israel befarech.

"**But** the Egyptians ill treated us and oppressed us and harshly enslaved us" (Deut. 26:6). "And the Egyptians illtreated us," as it is said (Ex.1:10), "Come and let us deal wisely with them lest they multiply and it come to pass that when there befalleth us any war, they ally themselves with our enemies and fight against us and flee the land." "And they afflicted us," and it is said (Ex. 1:11), "So they set taskmasters over them to oppress them with heavy burdens. And they built store-cities for Pharoah, Pithom and Rameses. "And they harshly enslaved us," as it is said (Ex. 1:13), "And they made the children of Israel to serve with rigor."

אֶל יְיָ אֱלֹהֵי אֲבוֹתֵינוּ וַיִּשְׁמַע
יְיָ אֶת קֹלֵנוּ, וַיַּרְא אֶת
עָנְיֵנוּ וְאֶת עֲמָלֵנוּ וְאֶת לַחֲצֵנוּ

כְּמָה שֶׁנֶּאֱמַר
וַיְהִי בַיָּמִים הָרַבִּים הָהֵם
וַיָּמָת מֶלֶךְ מִצְרַיִם וַיֵּאָנְחוּ
בְנֵי יִשְׂרָאֵל מִן הָעֲבֹדָה
וַיִּזְעָקוּ וַתַּעַל שַׁוְעָתָם אֶל
הָאֱלֹהִים מִן הָעֲבֹדָה

And we cried to the Lord, the God of our fathers, and the Lord heard our voice and saw our affliction, our toil and our oppression" (Deut. 26:7).

"And we cried to the Lord, the God of our fathers," as it is said (Ex. 2:23): "And it came to pass in the course of those many days that the king of Egypt died and the children of Israel sighed on account of their bondage and they cried and their crying came before God by reason of their bondage."

Va'nitzak el Adonay Elohei avoteinu, va'yishma Adonay et koleinu, va'yar et onyeinu ve'et amaleinu ve'et lachatzeinu.

"Va'nitzak el Adonay Elohei avoteinu," kema sheneemar: "va'yehi vayamim harabim ha'hem va'yamot melech Mitzrayim va'yeanchu venei Israel min ha'avoda va'yiz'aku va'taal shav'atam el ha'Elohim min ha'avoda."

וַיִּשְׁמַע אֶת קֹלֵנוּ

כְּמָה שֶׁנֶּאֱמַר וַיִּשְׁמַע אֱלֹהִים אֶת נַאֲקָתָם, וַיִּזְכֹּר אֱלֹהִים אֶת בְּרִיתוֹ אֶת אַבְרָהָם אֶת יִצְחָק וְאֶת יַעֲקֹב

"Va'yishma et koleinu," kema sheneemar: "va'yishma Elohim et naakatam, va'yizkor elohim et berito et Avraham et Yitzchak ve'et Yaacov."

"And the Lord heard our voice," as it is said (Ex. 2:24): "God heard their groaning and God remembered his covenant with Abraham, with Isaac and with Jacob."

וַיַּרְא אֶת עָנְיֵנוּ

זוֹ פְּרִישׁוּת דֶּרֶךְ אֶרֶץ כְּמָה שֶׁנֶּאֱמַר וַיַּרְא אֱלֹהִים אֶת בְּנֵי יִשְׂרָאֵל וַיֵּדַע אֱלֹהִים

"Va'yar et onyeinu," zo prishut derech eretz, kema sheneemar:" va'yar Elohim et benei Israel va'yeda Elohim."

"And he saw our affliction" refers to the enforced suspension of marital relations, as it is said (Ex. 2:25), "And God saw the children of Israel and God took cognizance of them."

וְאֶת עֲמָלֵנוּ

אֵלּוּ הַבָּנִים, כְּמָה שֶׁנֶּאֱמַר כָּל הַבֵּן הַיִּלּוֹד הַיְאֹרָה תַּשְׁלִיכֻהוּ וְכָל הַבַּת תְּחַיּוּן

"Ve'et amaleinu" elu ha'banim, kema sheneemar: "kol ha'ben hayilod ha'yeora tashlichuhu ve'chol ha'bat techayun."

"And our toil" refers to the drowning of the sons, as it is said, "Every boy that is born shall be thrown into the river but the girls shall be allowed to live" (Ex. 1:22).

וְאֶת לַחֲצֵנוּ

זֶה הַדֹּחַק כְּמָה שֶׁנֶּאֱמַר וְגַם רָאִיתִי אֶת הַלַּחַץ אֲשֶׁר מִצְרַיִם לֹחֲצִים אֹתָם

"Ve'et lachatzeinu" ze ha'dechak, kema sheneemar: ve'gam ra'iti et ha'lachatz asher Mitzrayim lochatzim otam."

"And our oppression" refers to the bitterness of slavery, as it is said (Ex. 3:9) "and now behold, the cry of the children of Israel is come to me, and also I have seen the oppression with which the Egyptians oppress them."

"And the Lord brought us
forth out of Egypt
with a mighty hand
and with an outstretched arm
with great terror
and with signs
and with wonders."

"Va'yotzienu Adonai
mi'Mitzrayim be'yad chazaka
u'vizeroa netuya u'vemora gadol
u'veotot u'vemoftim."

וַיּוֹצִאֵנוּ יְיָ מִמִּצְרַיִם.

לֹא עַל יְדֵי מַלְאָךְ וְלֹא עַל יְדֵי שָׂרָף וְלֹא עַל יְדֵי שָׁלִיחַ, אֶלָּא הַקָּדוֹשׁ בָּרוּךְ הוּא בִּכְבוֹדוֹ וּבְעַצְמוֹ, שֶׁנֶּאֱמַר: וְעָבַרְתִּי בְאֶרֶץ מִצְרַיִם בַּלַּיְלָה הַזֶּה וְהִכֵּיתִי כָל בְּכוֹר בְּאֶרֶץ מִצְרַיִם, מֵאָדָם וְעַד בְּהֵמָה, וּבְכָל אֱלֹהֵי מִצְרַיִם אֶעֱשֶׂה שְׁפָטִים אֲנִי יְיָ. וְעָבַרְתִּי בְאֶרֶץ מִצְרַיִם בַּלַּיְלָה הַזֶּה, אֲנִי וְלֹא מַלְאָךְ וְהִכֵּיתִי כָל בְּכוֹר בְּאֶרֶץ מִצְרַיִם, אֲנִי וְלֹא שָׂרָף וּבְכָל אֱלֹהֵי מִצְרַיִם אֶעֱשֶׂה שְׁפָטִים אֲנִי וְלֹא הַשָּׁלִיחַ. אֲנִי יְיָ. אֲנִי הוּא וְלֹא אַחֵר

"And the Lord brought us forth out of Egypt." Not by an angel, not by a seraph, not by a messenger, but the Holy One Himself, blessed be He in His glory, as it is written (Ex.12:12): "I will pass through the land of Egypt in that night and will smite every first-born in the land of Egypt, both man and beast, and against all the gods of Egypt I will execute judgement, I am the Lord." "I shall pass through the land of Egypt on that night," I, and not an angel. "And against all the gods of Egypt will I execute judgement": I, and not a messenger. "I the Lord, I am He and no other."

"Va'yotzienu Adonai mi'Mitzrayim" lo al yedei mal'ach ve'lo al yedei saraf ve'lo al yedei shaliach, ela ha'Kadosh Baruch Hu bichvodo u'veatzmo, shene'emar: ve'avarti be'eretz Mitzrayim balaila haze ve'hiketi chol bechor be'eretz Mitzrayim me'adam ve'ad behema u'vechol elohei Mitzrayim e'ese shefatim ani Adonay. "Ve'avarti be'eretz Mitzrayim balaila haze," ani ve'lo malach ve'hiketi kol bechor be'eretz Mitzrayim, ani ve'lo saraf, u'vechol elohei Mitzrayim e'ese shefatim ani ve'lo hashaliach, ani Adonay, ani hu ve'lo acher.

בְּיָד חֲזָקָה

זוֹ הַדֶּבֶר. כְּמָה שֶׁנֶּאֱמַר: הִנֵּה יַד יְיָ הוֹיָה בְּמִקְנְךָ אֲשֶׁר בַּשָּׂדֶה, בַּסּוּסִים, בַּחֲמוֹרִים, בַּגְּמַלִּים, בַּבָּקָר, וּבַצֹּאן, דֶּבֶר כָּבֵד מְאֹד

"With a mighty hand" refers to the pestilence, as it is said (Ex. 9:3): "Behold the hand of God is upon your livestock in the field, the horses, the asses, the camels, the cattle, and the sheep with a very severe pestilence."

"Be'yad chazaka" zo hadever, kema sheneemar: hine yad Adonay hoya bemiknecha asher basade basusim bachamorim bagemalim babakar ubatzon, dever kaved meod.

וּבִזְרֹעַ נְטוּיָה

זוֹ הַחֶרֶב. כְּמָה שֶׁנֶּאֱמַר: וְחַרְבּוֹ שְׁלוּפָה בְּיָדוֹ נְטוּיָה עַל יְרוּשָׁלָיִם.

"U'vizeroa netu'ya", zo ha'cherev, kema shene'emar: "ve'charbo shelufa be'yado netuya al yerushalaim."

"And with an outstretched arm" means the sword, as it is said (I Chron. 21:16), "With a drawn sword in his hand stretched over Jerusalem."

וּבְמוֹרָא גָּדוֹל

זֶה גִּלּוּי שְׁכִינָה. כְּמָה שֶׁנֶּאֱמַר: אוֹ הֲנִסָּה אֱלֹהִים לָבוֹא לָקַחַת לוֹ גוֹי מִקֶּרֶב גּוֹי בְּמַסֹּת, בְּאֹתֹת, וּבְמוֹפְתִים, וּבְמִלְחָמָה, וּבְיָד חֲזָקָה, וּבִזְרוֹעַ נְטוּיָה, וּבְמוֹרָאִים גְּדֹלִים, כְּכֹל אֲשֶׁר עָשָׂה לָכֶם יְיָ אֱלֹהֵיכֶם בְּמִצְרַיִם לְעֵינֶיךָ.

"U've'mora gadol," ze giluy shechina, kema shene'emar: "o ha'nisa Elohim lavo lakachat lo goy mikerev goy bemasot beotot u've'moftim u've'milchama u've'yad chazaka u'vezeiroa netuya u've'moraim gedolim ke'chol asher asa lachem Adonay eloheichem be'Mitzrayim le'eynecha."

"With great revelation" refers to the manifestation of the Divine Presence, as it is written (Deut. 4:34), "Or has any God ventured to go and take Him a nation from the midst of another nation by trials, by signs and wonders, by war and by a mighty hand and by an outstretched arm and by great terrors according to all that the Lord your God did for you in Egypt before your eyes."

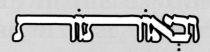

זֶה הַמַּטֶּה. כְּמָה שֶׁנֶּאֱמַר: וְאֶת הַמַּטֶּה הַזֶּה תִּקַּח בְּיָדְךָ אֲשֶׁר תַּעֲשֶׂה בּוֹ אֶת הָאֹתֹת.

"U've'otot" ze ha'mate, kema shene'emar: "ve'et ha'mate ha'ze tickach beyadecha asher taase bo et ha'otot."

"And with signs" refers to the rod, as it is said (Ex. 4:17), "And you Moses, shall take this rod in your hand, for with it you shall do the signs."

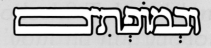

זֶה הַדָּם. כְּמָה שֶׁנֶּאֱמַר: וְנָתַתִּי מוֹפְתִים בַּשָּׁמַיִם וּבָאָרֶץ.

"U've'moftim" ze ha'dam, kema shene'emar: "ve'natati moftim ba'shamayim u'va'aretz."

"And with wonders" refers to the plague of blood, as it is said (Joel 3:3), "I will show portents in the heavens and on earth."

Blood, Fire and pillars of smoke

DAM
VA'ESH
VE'TIMROT ASHAN

Another explanation is as follows:

"With a strong hand" denotes two;
Davar acher: beyad chazaka-shtayim,

"With an outstretched arm" denotes two;
u'vizeroa netuya-shtayim,

"With great revelation" denotes two:
u'vemora gadol-shtayim,

"with signs" denotes two:
u'veotot-shtayim,

"with wonders" denotes two:
u'vemoftim-shtayim.

שֶׁהֵבִיא הַקָּדוֹשׁ בָּרוּךְ הוּא עַל הַמִּצְרִים בְּמִצְרַיִם, וְאֵלּוּ הֵן:

These are the ten plagues which the Holy One, Blessed be He, brought upon the Egyptians:

Elu eser makot shehevi ha'Kadosh Baruch Hu al ha'Mitzrim be'Mitzrayim. ve'elu hen:

DAM BLOOD

SHCHIN BOILS

TZFARDEA FROGS

BARAD HAIL

KINIM LICE

ARBE LOCUSTS

AROV BEASTS

CHOSHECH DARKNESS

DEVER PESTILENCE

**MAKAT BECHOROT
SLAYING OF THE FIRST-BORN**

רַבִּי יְהוּדָה הָיָה נוֹתֵן בָּהֶם סִימָנִים:

Rabbi Judah used to refer to them by mnemonics: detsa'h, adash, be'ah'ab

Rabi Yehuda haya noten bahem simanim: datzach adash be'achav

רַבִּי יוֹסֵי הַגְּלִילִי אוֹמֵר מִנַּיִן אַתָּה אוֹמֵר שֶׁלָּקוּ הַמִּצְרִים בְּמִצְרַיִם עֶשֶׂר מַכּוֹת וְעַל הַיָּם לָקוּ חֲמִשִּׁים מַכּוֹת בְּמִצְרַיִם מַה הוּא אוֹמֵר וַיֹּאמְרוּ הַחַרְטֻמִּים אֶל פַּרְעֹה אֶצְבַּע אֱלֹהִים הִוא וְעַל הַיָּם מַה הוּא אוֹמֵר וַיַּרְא יִשְׂרָאֵל אֶת הַיָּד הַגְּדוֹלָה אֲשֶׁר עָשָׂה יְיָ בְּמִצְרַיִם וַיִּירְאוּ הָעָם אֶת יְיָ וַיַּאֲמִינוּ בַּייָ וּבְמֹשֶׁה עַבְדּוֹ. כַּמָּה לָקוּ בְאֶצְבַּע עֶשֶׂר מַכּוֹת אֱמֹר מֵעַתָּה בְּמִצְרַיִם לָקוּ עֶשֶׂר מַכּוֹת וְעַל הַיָּם לָקוּ חֲמִשִּׁים מַכּוֹת

Rabi Yosei hagelili omer: minayin ata omer shelaku hamitzrim be'Mitzrayim eser makot, ve'al ha'yam laku chamishim makot. be'Mitzrayim ma hu omer: va'yomru ha'chartumim el Par'o: etzba Elohim hi Ve'al ha'yam ma hu omer: va'yar Israel et ha'yad ha'gedola asher asa Adonai be'Mitzrayim, va'yiruu ha'am et Adonay, va'ya'aminu ba' Adonai u've'Moshe avdo. Kama laku be'etzba, eser makot. Emor me'ata: be'Mitzrayim laku eser makot, ve'al ha'yam laku chamishim makot.

Rabbi Jose the Galilean asks: "How do we conclude that the Egyptians were afflicted with ten plagues in Egypt, but were stricken with fifty plagues at the Red Sea?" Of one of the plagues in Egypt, it is stated, "And the soothsayers said to Pharoah of the plague, 'This is the finger of God,'" (Ex.8:15), while at the Red Sea, it is stated: "And Israel saw the mighty hand with which the Lord had shown against the Egyptians and the people revered the Lord and believed in the Lord and had faith in his servant Moses" (Ex. 14:31). If one finger of God in Egypt caused ten plagues, we can assume that the whole hand of God at the Red Sea would have afflicted them with fifty plagues.

רַבִּי אֱלִיעֶזֶר אוֹמֵר מִנַּיִן שֶׁכָּל מַכָּה וּמַכָּה שֶׁהֵבִיא הַקָּדוֹשׁ בָּרוּךְ הוּא עַל הַמִּצְרִים בְּמִצְרַיִם הָיְתָה שֶׁל אַרְבַּע מַכּוֹת שֶׁנֶּאֱמַר יְשַׁלַּח בָּם חֲרוֹן אַפּוֹ עֶבְרָה וָזַעַם וְצָרָה מִשְׁלַחַת מַלְאֲכֵי רָעִים עֶבְרָה אַחַת וָזַעַם שְׁתַּיִם וְצָרָה שָׁלֹשׁ מִשְׁלַחַת מַלְאֲכֵי רָעִים אַרְבַּע אֱמֹר מֵעַתָּה בְּמִצְרַיִם לָקוּ אַרְבָּעִים מַכּוֹת וְעַל הַיָּם לָקוּ מָאתַיִם מַכּוֹת

Rabi Eliezer omer: minayin shekol maka u'maka she'hevi ha'Kadosh Baruch Hu al ha'mitzrim be'Mitzrayim hayta shel arba makot. Shene'emar, yeshalach bam charon apo, evra, va'zaam, ve'tzara, mishlachat malachei raim. evra-achat, vazaam-shtayim, vezara-shalosh, Mishlachat malachei raim-arba. Emor me'ata, be'Mitzrayim laku arbayim makot ve'al ha'yam laku matayim makot.

Rabbi Eliezer asks: "How can we prove that every plague brought by the Holy One, blessed be He, upon the Egyptians in Egypt consisted of four plages?" It is stated (Ps. 78:49): "He loosed upon the Egyptians the violence of his anger, wrath, indignation and ire, sending messengers of evil." According to this, each plague included: "anger," one; "wrath," two; "indignation and ire," three; and "sending messengers of evil," four. We assume, therefore, that in Egypt they were smitten with forty plagues, and at the Red Sea with two hundred plagues.

רַבִּי עֲקִיבָא אוֹמֵר

מִנַּיִן שֶׁכָּל מַכָּה וּמַכָּה שֶׁהֵבִיא הַקָּדוֹשׁ בָּרוּךְ הוּא עַל הַמִּצְרִים בְּמִצְרַיִם הָיְתָה שֶׁל חָמֵשׁ מַכּוֹת שֶׁנֶּאֱמַר יְשַׁלַּח בָּם חֲרוֹן אַפּוֹ עֶבְרָה וָזַעַם וְצָרָה מִשְׁלַחַת מַלְאֲכֵי רָעִים

חֲרוֹן אַפּוֹ, עֶבְרָה, וָזַעַם, וְצָרָה, מִשְׁלַחַת מַלְאֲכֵי רָעִים
אַחַת שְׁתַּיִם שָׁלוֹשׁ אַרְבַּע חָמֵשׁ
אֱמֹר מֵעַתָּה בְּמִצְרַיִם לָקוּ חֲמִשִּׁים מַכּוֹת
וְעַל הַיָּם לָקוּ חֲמִשִּׁים וּמָאתַיִם מַכּוֹת

Rabbi Akiba asks:

How can one know that every plague which the Holy One, blessed be He, brought upon the Egyptians was in fact five plagues? It is said (Ps. 78:49), "He loosed upon them the violence of his anger, wrath, indignation and ire, sending messengers of evil." Now "the violence of his anger" denotes one plague, "wrath" denotes two plagues, "indignation" denotes three plagues, "ire" denotes four plagues, "sending messengers of evil" denotes five plagues. We assume, therefore, that in Egypt the Egyptians were smitten with fifty plagues and at the Red Sea they were afflicted with two hundred and fifty plagues.

Rabi Akiva omer:

Minayin shekol maka umaka shehevi haKadosh Baruch Hu al ha'Mitzrim be'Mitzrayim hayta shel chamesh makot, sheneemar: yeshalach bam charon apo, evra, va'za'am, mishlachat malachei raim. Charon apo - achat, evra - shtayim, vazaam - shalosh, vetzara - arba, mishlachat malachei raim - chamesh. Emor me'ata be'Mitzrayim laku chamishim makot ve'al ha'yam laku chamishim u'matayim makot.

Many are The kindnesses God has bestowed upon us.

If he had brought us out of Egypt and not punished the Egyptians,
   it would have been enough.
If he had punished the Egyptians and not destroyed their gods,
   it would have been enough.
If he had destroyed their gods and not slain their first born,
   it would have been enough.
If he had slain their first-born, and not given us their substance,
   it would have been enough.
If he had given us their substance and not parted the sea for us,
   it would have been enough.
If he had parted the sea for us, and not led us across dry land,
   it would have been enough.
If he had led us across dry land, and not overwhelmed our adversaries in its midst,
   it would have been enough.
If he had overwhelmed our adversaries in its midst, and not satisfied our needs in the wilderness for forty years,
   it would have been enough.
If he had satisfied our needs in the wilderness for forty years, and not fed us with Manna,
   it would have been enough.
If he had fed us with Manna, and not given us the Shabbat,
   it would have been enough.
If he had given us the Shabbat, and not brought us near to Mount Sinai,
   it would have been enough.
If he had brought us near to Mount Sinai, and not given us the Torah,
   it would have been enough.
If he had given us the Torah and not led us into the Land of Israel,
   it would have been enough.
If he had let us into the Land of Israel and not built the Temple,
   it would have been enough.

כַּמָּה מַעֲלוֹת טוֹבוֹת לַמָּקוֹם עָלֵינוּ

אִלּוּ הוֹצִיאָנוּ מִמִּצְרַיִם	וְלֹא עָשָׂה בָהֶם שְׁפָטִים	דַּיֵּנוּ
אִלּוּ עָשָׂה בָהֶם שְׁפָטִים	וְלֹא עָשָׂה בֵאלֹהֵיהֶם	דַּיֵּנוּ
אִלּוּ עָשָׂה בֵאלֹהֵיהֶם	וְלֹא הָרַג אֶת בְּכוֹרֵיהֶם	דַּיֵּנוּ
אִלּוּ הָרַג אֶת בְּכוֹרֵיהֶם	וְלֹא נָתַן לָנוּ אֶת מָמוֹנָם	דַּיֵּנוּ
אִלּוּ נָתַן לָנוּ אֶת מָמוֹנָם	וְלֹא קָרַע לָנוּ אֶת הַיָּם	דַּיֵּנוּ
אִלּוּ קָרַע לָנוּ אֶת הַיָּם	וְלֹא הֶעֱבִירָנוּ בְתוֹכוֹ בֶּחָרָבָה	דַּיֵּנוּ
אִלּוּ הֶעֱבִירָנוּ בְתוֹכוֹ בֶּחָרָבָה	וְלֹא שִׁקַּע צָרֵינוּ בְּתוֹכוֹ	דַּיֵּנוּ
אִלּוּ שִׁקַּע צָרֵינוּ בְּתוֹכוֹ	וְלֹא סִפֵּק צָרְכֵּנוּ בַּמִּדְבָּר אַרְבָּעִים שָׁנָה	דַּיֵּנוּ
אִלּוּ סִפֵּק צָרְכֵּנוּ בַּמִּדְבָּר אַרְבָּעִים שָׁנָה	וְלֹא הֶאֱכִילָנוּ אֶת הַמָּן	דַּיֵּנוּ
אִלּוּ הֶאֱכִילָנוּ אֶת הַמָּן	וְלֹא נָתַן לָנוּ אֶת הַשַּׁבָּת	דַּיֵּנוּ
אִלּוּ נָתַן לָנוּ אֶת הַשַּׁבָּת	וְלֹא קֵרְבָנוּ לִפְנֵי הַר סִינַי	דַּיֵּנוּ
אִלּוּ קֵרְבָנוּ לִפְנֵי הַר סִינַי	וְלֹא נָתַן לָנוּ אֶת הַתּוֹרָה	דַּיֵּנוּ
אִלּוּ נָתַן לָנוּ אֶת הַתּוֹרָה	וְלֹא הִכְנִיסָנוּ לְאֶרֶץ יִשְׂרָאֵל	דַּיֵּנוּ
אִלּוּ הִכְנִיסָנוּ לְאֶרֶץ יִשְׂרָאֵל	וְלֹא בָנָה לָנוּ אֶת בֵּית הַבְּחִירָה	דַּיֵּנוּ

Kama ma'alot tovot la'makom aleinu

Illu hotzianu mi'Mitzrayim ve'lo asa bahem shefatim - dayennu

Illu asa bahem shefatim ve'lo asa veiloheihem - dayennu

Illu asa veiloheihem ve'lo harag et bechoreihem - dayennu

Illu harag et bechoreihem ve'lo natan lanu et mamonam - dayennu

Illu natan lanu et mamonam ve'lo kara lanu et ha'yam - dayennu

Illu kara lanu et ha'yam ve'he'eviranu ve'tocho becharava - dayennu

Illu he'eviranu ve'tocho becharava ve'lo shika tzareinu ve'tocho - dayennu

Illu shika tzareinu ve'tocho ve'lo sipek tzorkeinu bamidbar arbaim shana - dayennu

Illu sipek tzorkeinu bamidbar arbaim shana ve'lo he'echilanu et haman - dayennu

Illu he'echilanu et haman ve'lo natan lanu et ha'shabat - dayennu

Illu natan lanu et ha'shabat ve'lo kervanu lifnei har sinai - dayennu

Illu kervanu lifnei har sinai ve'lo natan lanu et ha'tora -dayennu

Illu natan lanu et ha'tora ve'lo hichnisanu le'Eretz Israel - dayennu

Illu hichnisanu le'Eretz Israel ve'lo bana lanu et beit ha'bechira - dayennu

עַל אַחַת כַּמָּה וְכַמָּה טוֹבָה כְפוּלָה וּמְכֻפֶּלֶת לַמָּקוֹם עָלֵינוּ: שֶׁהוֹצִיאָנוּ מִמִּצְרַיִם, וְעָשָׂה בָהֶם שְׁפָטִים, וְעָשָׂה בֵאלֹהֵיהֶם, וְהָרַג אֶת בְּכוֹרֵיהֶם, וְנָתַן לָנוּ אֶת מָמוֹנָם, וְקָרַע לָנוּ אֶת הַיָּם, וְהֶעֱבִירָנוּ בְתוֹכוֹ בֶּחָרָבָה, וְשִׁקַּע צָרֵינוּ בְּתוֹכוֹ, וְסִפֵּק צָרְכֵּנוּ בַּמִּדְבָּר אַרְבָּעִים שָׁנָה, וְהֶאֱכִילָנוּ אֶת הַמָּן, וְנָתַן לָנוּ אֶת הַשַּׁבָּת, וְקֵרְבָנוּ לִפְנֵי הַר סִינַי, וְנָתַן לָנוּ אֶת הַתּוֹרָה, וְהִכְנִיסָנוּ לְאֶרֶץ יִשְׂרָאֵל, וּבָנָה לָנוּ אֶת בֵּית הַבְּחִירָה לְכַפֵּר עַל כָּל עֲוֹנוֹתֵינוּ.

How greatly the goodness of the Almighty has been doubled and redoubled towards us! He brought us out of Egypt and wrought judgement upon the Egyptians, smote their gods, and slew their first-born and gave us their substance and divided the sea for us and caused us to pass through it on dry land and overwhelmed our enemies in its midst and satisfied our needs in the desert for forty years and fed us with Manna and gave us the Sabbath and brought us near to Mount Sinai and gave us the Torah and built the Temple to enable us to atone for all our sins.

Al achat kama ve'chama tova kefula u'mechupelet la'makom aleinu - shehotzianu mimitzrayim, ve'asa vahem shefatim, ve'asa ve'eloheihem, ve'harag et bechoreihem, ve'natan lanu et mamonam, ve'kara lanu et ha'yam, ve'he'eviranu ve'tocho be'horava, ve'shika tzareinu be'tocho, ve'sipek tzorcheinu bamidbar arbaim shana, ve'he'echilanu et haman, ve'natan lanu et ha'shabat, ve'kervanu lifnei har sinai, ve'natan lanu et ha'tora, ve'hichnisanu le'Eretz Israel, u'vana lanu et beit habechira lechaper al kol avonoteinu.

רַבָּן גַּמְלִיאֵל הָיָה אוֹמֵר: כָּל מִי שֶׁלֹּא אָמַר שְׁלֹשָׁה דְבָרִים אֵלּוּ בַּפֶּסַח, לֹא יָצָא יְדֵי חוֹבָתוֹ, וְאֵלּוּ הֵן

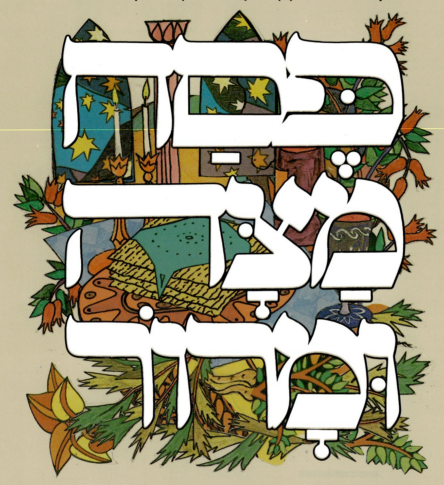

פֶּסַח מַצָּה וּמָרוֹר

Rabban Gamliel used to say:
whoever does not mention these three things on Passover has not fulfilled his duty. The three things are: the Paschal Lamb, the unleavened bread and the bitter herbs.

Raban Gamliel haya omer: kol mi shelo amar shelosha devarim elu ba'pesach, lo yatza yedei chovato, ve'elu hen: pesach, matza, umaror.

שֶׁהָיוּ אֲבוֹתֵינוּ אוֹכְלִים בִּזְמַן שֶׁבֵּית הַמִּקְדָּשׁ הָיָה קַיָּם עַל שׁוּם מָה? עַל שׁוּם שֶׁפָּסַח הַקָּדוֹשׁ בָּרוּךְ הוּא עַל בָּתֵּי אֲבוֹתֵינוּ בְּמִצְרַיִם שֶׁנֶּאֱמַר: וַאֲמַרְתֶּם זֶבַח פֶּסַח הוּא לַיְיָ, אֲשֶׁר פָּסַח עַל בָּתֵּי בְנֵי יִשְׂרָאֵל בְּמִצְרַיִם, בְּנָגְפּוֹ אֶת מִצְרַיִם וְאֶת בָּתֵּינוּ הִצִּיל וַיִּקֹּד הָעָם וַיִּשְׁתַּחֲווּ.

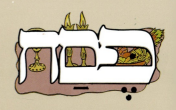

Pesach she'hayu avoteinu ochlim bizman shebeit ha'mikdash haya kayam al shum ma? al shum she'pasach ha'Kadosh Baruch Hu al batei avoteinu be'Mitzrayim shene'emar: va'amartem zevach pesach hu la'Adonay asher pasach al batei venei Israel be'Mitzraim benagpo et Mitzrayim ve'et bateinu hitzil va'yikod ha'am va'yishtachavu.

Why did our fathers eat the Paschal offering, during the days when the Temple existed? Because the Holy One, Blessed be He, passed over the houses of our fathers in Egypt, as it is said (Ex. 12:27), "And you shall say: It is the Passover sacrifice for The Lord who passed over the houses of the children of Israel in Egypt when he smote the Egyptians and spared our homes. And the people bowed their heads and worshipped."

זוֹ שֶׁאָנוּ אוֹכְלִים עַל שׁוּם מָה? עַל שׁוּם שֶׁלֹּא הִסְפִּיק בְּצֵקָם שֶׁל אֲבוֹתֵינוּ לְהַחֲמִיץ, עַד שֶׁנִּגְלָה עֲלֵיהֶם מֶלֶךְ מַלְכֵי הַמְּלָכִים הַקָּדוֹשׁ בָּרוּךְ הוּא וּגְאָלָם. שֶׁנֶּאֱמַר: וַיֹּאפוּ אֶת הַבָּצֵק אֲשֶׁר הוֹצִיאוּ מִמִּצְרַיִם, עֻגֹת מַצּוֹת, כִּי לֹא חָמֵץ, כִּי גֹרְשׁוּ מִמִּצְרַיִם וְלֹא יָכְלוּ לְהִתְמַהְמֵהַּ, וְגַם צֵדָה לֹא עָשׂוּ לָהֶם.

This unleavened bread that we eat, what is it for? It is because there was no time for the dough of our fathers in Egypt to become leavened before the King of Kings, the Holy One, Blessed be He, revealed Himself to them and redeemed them. As it is said (Ex. 12:39), "And they baked unleavened bread that they brought forth from Egypt because there was no leaven; for they had been thrust out of Egypt and could not tarry, neither had they time to prepare food for their journey."

Matza zo she'anu ochlim al shum ma? al shum she'lo hispik betzekam shel avoteinu le'hachmitz ad shenigla aleihem melech malchei ha'melachim, ha'Kadosh Baruch Hu u'gealam, shene'emar: va'yofu et habatzek asher hotziu mi'Mitzrayim ugot matzot ki lo chametz, ki gorshu mi'Mitzrayim ve'lo yachlu le'hitmahameha ve'gam tzeida lo asu lahem.

זֶה שֶׁאָנוּ אוֹכְלִים עַל שׁוּם מָה? עַל שׁוּם שֶׁמֵּרְרוּ הַמִּצְרִים אֶת חַיֵּי אֲבוֹתֵינוּ בְּמִצְרַיִם שֶׁנֶּאֱמַר: וַיְמָרְרוּ אֶת חַיֵּיהֶם בַּעֲבֹדָה קָשָׁה בְּחֹמֶר וּבִלְבֵנִים וּבְכָל עֲבֹדָה בַּשָּׂדֶה. אֶת כָּל עֲבֹדָתָם אֲשֶׁר עָבְדוּ בָהֶם בְּפָרֶךְ.

The Bitter Herb that we eat, what is it for? Because the Egyptians embittered the lives of our fathers in Egypt, as it is said (Ex. 1:14), "And they embittered their lives with cruel servitude, setting them to work with mortar and bricks and all kinds of work in the field and the forced labor and servitude they performed with rigor."

Maror ze she'anu ochlim al shum ma? al shum she'mereru ha'Mitzrim et chayei avoteinu be'Mitzrayim, shene'emar: va'yemareru et chayeihem ba'avoda kasha bechomer u'vilvenim u've'chol avoda ba'sade, et kol avodatam asher avdu vahem be'farech.

בְּכָל דּוֹר וָדוֹר חַיָּב אָדָם לִרְאוֹת אֶת עַצְמוֹ כְּאִלּוּ הוּא יָצָא מִמִּצְרַיִם

שֶׁנֶּאֱמַר: וְהִגַּדְתָּ לְבִנְךָ בַּיּוֹם הַהוּא לֵאמֹר: בַּעֲבוּר זֶה עָשָׂה יְיָ לִי בְּצֵאתִי מִמִּצְרָיִם. לֹא אֶת אֲבוֹתֵינוּ בִּלְבָד גָּאַל הַקָּדוֹשׁ בָּרוּךְ הוּא אֶלָּא אַף אוֹתָנוּ גָּאַל עִמָּהֶם. שֶׁנֶּאֱמַר: וְאוֹתָנוּ הוֹצִיא מִשָּׁם לְמַעַן הָבִיא אֹתָנוּ לָתֶת לָנוּ אֶת הָאָרֶץ אֲשֶׁר נִשְׁבַּע לַאֲבוֹתֵינוּ.

In every generation it is a person's duty to consider himself as if he personally had come forth from Egypt, as it is said (Ex. 13:8), "On that day you shall tell your son, saying, it is because of what the Lord did for me when I came forth out of Egypt." For it was not our forefathers alone that the Holy One, Blessed be He, redeemed, but us as well, as it is said (Deut. 6:23), "And he led us out of there to lead us to the land and to give us the land which He swore to our fathers."

Bechol dor va'dor chayav adam lir'ot et atzmo ke'ilu hu yatza mi'Mitzraim. She'neemar: ve'higadta levincha bayom ha'hu le'emor: ba'avur ze asa Adonay li betzeti mi'Mitzraim, lo et avoteinu bilvad ga'al ha'Kadosh Baruch Hu, ela af otanu ga'al imahem. Shene'emar: ve'otanu hotzi misham le'maan havi otanu latet lanu et ha'aretz asher nishba la'avoteinu.

The Matzah is covered and the cup of wine is raised   מכסה את המצות ואוחז הכוס בידו

לְפִיכָךְ אֲנַחְנוּ חַיָּבִים לְהוֹדוֹת, לְהַלֵּל, לְשַׁבֵּחַ, לְפָאֵר, לְרוֹמֵם, לְהַדֵּר, לְבָרֵךְ, לְעַלֵּה, וּלְקַלֵּס, לְמִי שֶׁעָשָׂה לַאֲבוֹתֵינוּ אֶת כָּל-הַנִּסִּים הָאֵלוּ. הוֹצִיאָנוּ מֵעַבְדוּת לְחֵרוּת, מִיָּגוֹן לְשִׂמְחָה, מֵאֵבֶל לְיוֹם טוֹב, וּמֵאֲפֵלָה לְאוֹר גָּדוֹל, וּמִשִּׁעְבּוּד לִגְאֻלָּה, וְנֹאמַר לְפָנָיו שִׁירָה חֲדָשָׁה,

Accordingly it is our duty to thank, praise, laud, glorify, exalt, honor, bless, and extol Him who wrought all these miracles for our fathers and for us. He brought us forth from bondage to freedom, from grief to joy, from mourning to festivity, from darkness to great light, and from subjection to redemption. Let us, therefore, sing before Him.
Hallelujah. Praise the Lord.

Lefichach anachnu chayavim le'hodot le'halel le'shabe'ach, le'faer, le'romem, le'hader, le'varech, le'ale, u'le'kales lemi she'asa la'avoteinu et kol ha'nisim ha'elu. Hotzianu me'avdut le'cherut, mi'yagon le'simcha, me'evel le'yom tov, u'me'afela le'or gadol, u'mishiabud li'geula. Ve'nomar lefanav shira hadasha. Haleluyah.

Put down the cup and continue

ניח את הכוס מידו ואמר:

הַ‏לְלוּיָהּ הַלְלוּ עַבְדֵי יְיָ: הַלְלוּ אֶת שֵׁם יְיָ: יְהִי שֵׁם יְיָ מְבוֹרָךְ מֵעַתָּה וְעַד עוֹלָם: מִמִּזְרַח שֶׁמֶשׁ עַד מְבוֹאוֹ מְהֻלָּל שֵׁם יְיָ: רָם עַל כָּל גּוֹיִם יְיָ עַל הַשָּׁמַיִם כְּבוֹדוֹ: מִי כַּייָ אֱלֹהֵינוּ הַמַּגְבִּיהִי לָשָׁבֶת: הַמַּשְׁפִּילִי לִרְאוֹת בַּשָּׁמַיִם וּבָאָרֶץ: מְקִימִי מֵעָפָר דָּל מֵאַשְׁפּוֹת יָרִים אֶבְיוֹן: לְהוֹשִׁיבִי עִם נְדִיבִים עִם נְדִיבֵי עַמּוֹ: מוֹשִׁיבִי עֲקֶרֶת הַבַּיִת אֵם הַבָּנִים שְׂמֵחָה הַלְלוּיָהּ:

Hallelujah - Praise the Lord. Praise the Lord, you servants of the Lord, praise the name of the Lord. Blessed be the name of the Lord. From the rising of the sun to its setting may the Lord's name be praised. The Lord is high above all nations, His glory is above the heavens. Who is like the Lord our God, Who dwells so high, Who looks down upon heaven and earth, Who raises up the poor from the dust. He lifts the needy from the dunghill; to set him with princes, with the princes of his people, Who makes the barren woman dwell in her house, as a joyful mother of children. Praise ye the Lord.

Haleluya halelu avdei Adonay halelu et shem Adonay: ye'hi shem Adonay mevorach me'ata ve'ad olam: mimizrach shemesh ad mevo'o mehulal shem Adonay: ram al kol goyim Adonay al ha'shamayim kevodo: mi ka'Adonay eloheinu ha'magbihi lashavet: ha'mashpili lir'ot bashamayim u'va'aretz: mekimi me'afar dal me'ashpot yarim evyon: le'hoshivi im nedivim im nedivei amo: moshivi akeret ha'bayit em ha'banim semecha haleluya.

בְּצֵאת יִשְׂרָאֵל מִמִּצְרָיִם בֵּית יַעֲקֹב מֵעַם לֹעֵז: הָיְתָה יְהוּדָה לְקָדְשׁוֹ יִשְׂרָאֵל מַמְשְׁלוֹתָיו: הַיָּם רָאָה וַיָּנֹס הַיַּרְדֵּן יִסֹּב לְאָחוֹר: הֶהָרִים רָקְדוּ כְאֵילִים גְּבָעוֹת כִּבְנֵי צֹאן: מַה לְּךָ הַיָּם כִּי תָנוּס הַיַּרְדֵּן תִּסֹּב לְאָחוֹר: הֶהָרִים תִּרְקְדוּ כְאֵילִים גְּבָעוֹת כִּבְנֵי צֹאן: מִלִּפְנֵי אָדוֹן חוּלִי אָרֶץ מִלִּפְנֵי אֱלוֹהַּ יַעֲקֹב: הַהֹפְכִי הַצּוּר אֲגַם מָיִם חַלָּמִישׁ לְמַעְיְנוֹ מָיִם

Be'tzet Israel mi'Mitzrayim beit Yaakov meam loez; hayta Yehuda lekodsho, Israel mamshelotav: hayam ra'a va'yanos ha'Yarden yisov le'achor: he'harim rakdu che'eilim gevaot kivnei tzon: ma lecha hayam ki tanus ha'yarden tisov le'achor he'harim tirkedu che'eilim gevaot kivnei tzom milifnei Adon chuli aretz milifnei Eloha Yaakov: ha'hofchi hatzur agam mayim, chalamish le'ma'ayno mayim.

When Israel came out of Egypt, the house of Jacob from a people of a foreign language; Judah became his sanctuary, Israel his dominion. The sea looked and fled; the Jordan turned back. The mountains skipped like rams, the hills like lambs. What happened to you, sea? Why did you turn back? Why skip like rams, you mountains, and hills like lambs? Tremble, earth, at the presence of the Lord, at the presence of the God of Jacob, Who turns the rock into a pool of water, the flint-rock into a fountain of water. (Psalm 114)

Raise the cup of wine and say:

מגביה את הכוס ואומר:

בָּרוּךְ אַתָּה יְיָ, אֱלֹהֵינוּ מֶלֶךְ הָעוֹלָם, אֲשֶׁר גְּאָלָנוּ וְגָאַל אֶת אֲבוֹתֵינוּ מִמִּצְרַיִם, וְהִגִּיעָנוּ הַלַּיְלָה הַזֶּה לֶאֱכָל בּוֹ מַצָּה וּמָרוֹר. כֵּן יְיָ אֱלֹהֵינוּ וֵאלֹהֵי אֲבוֹתֵינוּ יַגִּיעֵנוּ לְמוֹעֲדִים וְלִרְגָלִים אֲחֵרִים הַבָּאִים לִקְרָאתֵנוּ לְשָׁלוֹם, שְׂמֵחִים בְּבִנְיַן עִירֶךָ וְשָׂשִׂים בַּעֲבוֹדָתֶךָ, וְנֹאכַל שָׁם מִן הַזְּבָחִים וּמִן הַפְּסָחִים אֲשֶׁר יַגִּיעַ דָּמָם עַל קִיר מִזְבַּחֲךָ לְרָצוֹן, וְנוֹדֶה לְךָ שִׁיר חָדָשׁ עַל גְּאֻלָּתֵנוּ וְעַל פְּדוּת נַפְשֵׁנוּ. בָּרוּךְ אַתָּה יְיָ, גָּאַל יִשְׂרָאֵל.

BLESSED ARE YOU, LORD OUR GOD, KING OF THE UNIVERSE, WHO HAS REDEEMED OUR FATHERS FROM EGYPT AND ENABLED US TO REACH THIS NIGHT TO EAT UNLEAVENED BREAD AND BITTER HERB LORD, OUR GOD AND GOD OF OUR FATHERS, ENABLE US TO REACH TO OTHER APPOINTED TIMES AND FESTIVALS IN PEACE, REJOICING IN THE REBUILDING OF YOUR CITY AND JOYFUL IN YOUR SERVICE. THEN WE SHALL PARTAKE OF THE SACRIFICE AND THE PASCHAL LAMBS, WHOSE BLOOD WILL REACH THE SIDE OF YOUR ALTAR FOR ACCEPTANCE. AND WE SHALL SING YOU A NEW SONG IN GRATITUDE FOR OUR REDEMPTION AND FOR THE DELIVERENCE OF OUR SOUL. BLESSED ARE YOU, LORD, WHO HAS REDEEMED ISRAEL.

Baruch ata Adonay, eloheinu melech ha'olam, asher gealanu ve'gaal et avoteinu mi'Mitzrayim, ve'higianu ha'layla haze le'echol bo matza u'maror. Ken Adonay eloheinu vei'lohei avoteinu yagienu lemoadim ve'liregalim acherim habaim likratenu le'shalom, semechim be'vinyan irecha, ve'sasim ba'avodatecha. Ve'nochal sham min ha'zevachim u'min ha'pesachim asher yagia damam al kir mizbachacha le'ratzon, ve'node lecha shir chadash al geulateinu ve'al pedut nafsheinu Baruch ata Adonay, gaal Israel.

BLESSED ARE YOU, LORD OUR GOD, KING OF THE UNIVERSE,
WHO CREATED THE FRUIT OF THE VINE.

Baruch ata Adonay, eloheinu melech ha'olam, bore peri ha'gafen.

Drink the second cup of wine while leaning to the left

שותים כוס בהסבת שמאל

רָחְצָה

נוטלים את הידים לסעודה
Wash the hands and say:

בָּרוּךְ אַתָּה יְיָ אֱלֹהֵינוּ מֶלֶךְ הָעוֹלָם אֲשֶׁר קִדְּשָׁנוּ בְּמִצְוֹתָיו וְצִוָּנוּ עַל נְטִילַת יָדָיִם

מוֹצִיא מַצָּה

לוקחים את המצות ביד
Holding all three matzot

הנני מוכן ומזומן לקיים מצות אכילת מצה. לשם יחוד קודשא בריך הוא ושכינתיה על ידי ההוא טמיר ונעלם בשם כל ישראל

בָּרוּךְ אַתָּה יְיָ אֱלֹהֵינוּ מֶלֶךְ הָעוֹלָם הַמּוֹצִיא לֶחֶם מִן הָאָרֶץ

מניחים את המצה התחתונה ואוחזים את העליונה והאמצעית

בָּרוּךְ אַתָּה יְיָ אֱלֹהֵינוּ מֶלֶךְ הָעוֹלָם, אֲשֶׁר קִדְּשָׁנוּ בְּמִצְוֹתָיו וְצִוָּנוּ עַל אֲכִילַת מַצָּה

אוכלים בהסבה כזית אחת מכל משתי המצות שביד, ביחד.
Holding only the top and broken middle Matza

RACHZA

Baruch ata Adonay, eloheinu melech ha'olam, asher kidshanu bemitzvotav ve'tzivanu al netilat yadayim.

Blessed are You, Lord our God, King of the Universe, Who has sanctified us by Your commandments, and enjoined on us the washing of the hands.

MOTZI

Baruch ata, Adonay, eloheinu melech ha'olam, ha'motzi lechem min ha'aretz.

Blessed are You, Lord our God, King of the Universe, Who brings forth bread from the earth.

MATZA

Baruch ata, Adonay, eloheinu melech ha'olam, asher kidshanu bemitzvotav ve'tzivanu al achilat matza.

Blessed are You, Lord our God, King of the Universe, Who has sanctified us by Your commandments, and enjoined on us eating unleavened bread.

מָרוֹר

לוקחים כזית מרור טובלים בחרוסת

הֲרֵינִי מוּכָן וּמְזֻמָּן לְקַיֵּם מִצְוַת אֲכִילַת מָרוֹר לְשֵׁם יִחוּד קֻדְשָׁא בְּרִיךְ הוּא וּשְׁכִינְתֵּיהּ עַל יְדֵי הַהוּא טָמִיר וְנֶעְלָם בְּשֵׁם כָּל יִשְׂרָאֵל

Dip bitter herbs in haroseth and say:

בָּרוּךְ אַתָּה יְיָ אֱלֹהֵינוּ מֶלֶךְ הָעוֹלָם אֲשֶׁר קִדְּשָׁנוּ בְּמִצְוֹתָיו וְצִוָּנוּ עַל אֲכִילַת מָרוֹר

אוכלים בלא הסבה

כּוֹרֵךְ

קודם לאכילה אומרים

בוצעים מהמצה התחתונה כזית וכורך עמה כזית מן המרור ואוכלים ביחד בהסבה

זֵכֶר לְמִקְדָּשׁ כְּהִלֵּל. כֵּן עָשָׂה הִלֵּל בִּזְמַן שֶׁבֵּית הַמִּקְדָּשׁ הָיָה קַיָּם, הָיָה כּוֹרֵךְ (פֶּסַח) מַצָּה וּמָרוֹר וְאוֹכֵל בְּיַחַד, לְקַיֵּם מַה שֶּׁנֶּאֱמַר: עַל מַצּוֹת וּמְרוֹרִים יֹאכְלֻהוּ

Eat a sandwich of bitter herbs between two pieces of the bottom Matza.

אוכלים ושותים כברכת ה' נוהגים לאכול ביצה קשה לפני סעודת החג

Baruch ata, Adonay, eloheinu melech ha'olam, asher kidshanu bemitzvotav ve'tzivanu al achilat maror.

Zecher lemikdash ke'Hillel. Ken asa Hillel bizman shebeit ha'mikdash haya kayam, haya korech (pesach) matza u'maror ve'ochel be'yachad, lekayem ma shene'emar: al matzot u'merorim yochluhu.

MAROR

Blessed are You, Lord our God, King of the Universe, Who has sanctified us by His commandments and enjoined on us the eating of the bitter herb.

KORECH

This is in commemoration of the Temple according to the custom of Hillel. For Hillel during the time when the Temple was still standing, used to combine unleavened bread with bitter herb and eat them together, in fulfillment of the verse (Num. 9:11), "With unleavened bread and bitter herbs shall they eat it."

SHULCHAN ORECH

The festive meal, according to God's blessing. A hard cooked egg is customarily eaten first.

הנני מוכן ומזומן לקיים מצות אכילת אפיקומן לשם יחוד קודשא בריך הוא ושכינתיה על ידי ההוא טמיר ונעלם בשם כל ישראל.

בגמר הסעודה אוכלים בהסבה כשני זיתים מהמצה שהצפינו לאפיקומן.
At the end of the meal while reclining to the left, eat the portion of two olives from the Afikoman

TZAFUN
I stand ready to fulfill the commandment of the eating of Afikoman. In the name of the Lord who has spread His mantle of glory over His people Israel.

Hineni muchan u'mezuman lekayem mitzvat achilat afikoman leshem yichud Kudsha, Brich Hu u'shechintei al yedey ha'hu tamir ve'neelam beshem kol Israel.

הנני מוכן ומזומן לקיים מצות עשה של ברכת המזון כמו שכתוב בתורה: ואכלת ושבעת וברכת את יי אלודיך על הארץ הטובה אשר נתן לך. לשם יחוד קודשא בריך הוא ושכינתיה על ידי ההוא טמיר ונעלם בשם כל ישראל.
(שלשה שאכלו כאחד חייבים לזמן).

מוזגין כוס שלישי ונוטלין מים אחרונים.
Pour the third cup of wine, and wash with finger bowl water

BARECH
I stand ready to fulfill the commandment of Grace after Meals. As it is written in the Tora: "You have eaten and been satisfied and you shall bless the Lord your God for the bountiful land He has given you." In the name of the Lord who has spread His mantle of glory over His people Israel."

Hineni muchan u'mezuman lekayem mitzvat ase shel birkat hamazon kemo shekatuv batora: ve'achalta ve'savata u'verachta et Adonay eloheicha al ha'aretz hatova asher natan lecha. Leshem Kudsha Brich Hu' u'shchintei al yedei ha'hu tamir ve'neelam beshem kol israel.

שִׁיר הַמַּעֲלוֹת

בְּשׁוּב יְיָ אֶת־שִׁיבַת צִיּוֹן הָיִינוּ כְּחֹלְמִים:
אָז יִמָּלֵא שְׂחוֹק פִּינוּ וּלְשׁוֹנֵנוּ רִנָּה,
אָז יֹאמְרוּ בַגּוֹיִם הִגְדִּיל יְיָ לַעֲשׂוֹת עִם־אֵלֶּה,
הִגְדִּיל יְיָ לַעֲשׂוֹת עִמָּנוּ הָיִינוּ שְׂמֵחִים.
שׁוּבָה יְיָ אֶת־שְׁבוּתֵנוּ כַּאֲפִיקִים בַּנֶּגֶב:
הַזֹּרְעִים בְּדִמְעָה בְּרִנָּה יִקְצֹרוּ.
הָלוֹךְ יֵלֵךְ וּבָכֹה נֹשֵׂא מֶשֶׁךְ הַזָּרַע.
בֹּא־יָבֹא בְרִנָּה נֹשֵׂא אֲלֻמֹּתָיו:

A song of Ascents: When the Lord brought the exiles back to Zion, we were like dreamers. Then were our mouths filled with laughter and our tongues with joyous singing. Then it was said among the nations: "The Lord has done great and wondrous things for them." Indeed the Lord had done marvelous deeds for us and we rejoiced. Bring our exiles out of captivity, Oh Lord, like streams of water in the Negev: for he who sows with tears will reap with joy, and he who has taken his seed to the field and has wept, will return with joy, bearing the sheaves of his harvest.

Shir ha'ma'alot beshuv Adonai et shivat Tzion hayianu kecholmim: Az yimale sechok pinu u'leshonenu rina. Az yomru bagoyim higdil Adonay la'asot im ele, higdil Adonay la'asot imanu hayinu semechim. Shuva Adonay et shevutenu ka'afikim banegev: ha'zorim bedimaa berina yiktzoru. Haloch yelech u'vacho noseh meshech ha'zara. Bo yavo berina nose alumotav.

Leader: Let us chant the blessing.
All: Bless the Lord's name now and forever.
Leader: We shall bless the Lord for we have partaken of His bounty.
All: Bless the Lord, of Whose bounty we have partaken and by Whose grace we live.
Leader: Bless the Lord.

הַמְזַמֵן אוֹמֵר: רַבּוֹתַי נְבָרֵךְ.
הַמְסֻבִּים עוֹנִים: יְהִי שֵׁם יְיָ מְבֹרָךְ מֵעַתָּה וְעַד עוֹלָם.
הַמְזַמֵן: בִּרְשׁוּת מָרָנָן וְרַבּוֹתַי, נְבָרֵךְ [אֱלֹהֵינוּ] שֶׁאָכַלְנוּ מִשֶּׁלוֹ.
הַמְסֻבִּים: בָּרוּךְ [אֱלֹהֵינוּ] שֶׁאָכַלְנוּ מִשֶּׁלוֹ וּבְטוּבוֹ חָיִינוּ.
הַמְזַמֵן: בָּרוּךְ [אֱלֹהֵינוּ] שֶׁאָכַלְנוּ מִשֶּׁלוֹ וּבְטוּבוֹ חָיִינוּ.

(Ha'mezamen omer): Rabotai nevarech.
(Ha'mesubim onim): Yehi shem Adonay mevorach me'ata ve'ad olam.
Hamezamen: Birshut maranan ve'rabotay, nevarech eloheinu she'achalnu mishelo.
Ha'mesubim: Baruch eloheinu sheachalnu mishelo u'vetuvo chayinu.
Hamezamen: Baruch eloheinu sheachalnu mishelo u'vetuvo chayinu.

בָּרוּךְ אַתָּה, יְיָ, אֱלֹהֵינוּ מֶלֶךְ הָעוֹלָם, הַזָּן אֶת הָעוֹלָם כֻּלּוֹ בְּטוּבוֹ, בְּחֵן בְּחֶסֶד וּבְרַחֲמִים, הוּא נוֹתֵן לֶחֶם לְכָל בָּשָׂר, כִּי לְעוֹלָם חַסְדּוֹ. וּבְטוּבוֹ הַגָּדוֹל תָּמִיד לֹא חָסַר לָנוּ, וְאַל יֶחְסַר לָנוּ מָזוֹן לְעוֹלָם וָעֶד. בַּעֲבוּר שְׁמוֹ הַגָּדוֹל, כִּי הוּא אֵל זָן וּמְפַרְנֵס לַכֹּל, וּמֵטִיב לַכֹּל, וּמֵכִין מָזוֹן לְכָל בְּרִיּוֹתָיו אֲשֶׁר בָּרָא. בָּרוּךְ אַתָּה יְיָ הַזָּן אֶת הַכֹּל.

Blessed are You, Lord our God, King of the Universe, Who nourishes all the world with His goodness, kindness and compassion. He gives food to all living creatures, for His loving-kindness is eternal. And because of His great goodness we have never lacked sustenance and never will for all time. It is He who feeds us and sustains us all; His table is set for all, and He provides sustenance for all. Blessed are You, Oh Lord, Who nourishes all the universe.

Baruch ata Adonay, eloheinu melech ha'olam, ha'zan et ha'olam kulo be'tuvo, be'chen be'chesed u'verachamim, hu noten lechem lechol basar, ki le'olam chasdo. U'vetuvo ha'gadol tamid lo chasar lanu, ve'al yechsar lanu mazon le'olam va'ed. Ba'avur shemo ha'gadol, ki hu el zan u'mefarnes lakol, u'meitiv lakol, u'mechin mazon lechol beriyotav asher bara. Baruch ata Adonay ha'zan et ha'kol.

נוֹדֶה לְךָ, יְיָ אֱלֹהֵינוּ, עַל שֶׁהִנְחַלְתָּ לַאֲבוֹתֵינוּ אֶרֶץ חֶמְדָּה טוֹבָה וּרְחָבָה, וְעַל שֶׁהוֹצֵאתָנוּ, יְיָ אֱלֹהֵינוּ מֵאֶרֶץ מִצְרַיִם, וּפְדִיתָנוּ מִבֵּית עֲבָדִים, וְעַל בְּרִיתְךָ שֶׁחָתַמְתָּ בִּבְשָׂרֵנוּ, וְעַל תּוֹרָתְךָ שֶׁלִּמַּדְתָּנוּ, וְעַל חֻקֶּיךָ שֶׁהוֹדַעְתָּנוּ, וְעַל חַיִּים חֵן וָחֶסֶד שֶׁחוֹנַנְתָּנוּ, וְעַל אֲכִילַת מָזוֹן שֶׁאַתָּה זָן וּמְפַרְנֵס אוֹתָנוּ תָּמִיד בְּכָל יוֹם וּבְכָל עֵת וּבְכָל שָׁעָה.

We give thanks to You, Lord our God, for the legacy of a beautiful and spacious land, for the covenant and the Torah, and for taking us out of slavery in Egypt. And for the covenant of the flesh and all the laws and statutes You have given us. And for the life, grace and mercy that you have graciously besto upon us. And we thank You for the food which sustains our lives.

Node lecha Adonai eloheinu, al she'hinchalta la'avoteinu eretz chemda tova u'rechava, ve'al she'hotzetanu, Adonay eloheinu me'eretz Mitzrayim, u'feditanu mibeit avadim, ve'al beritcha she'chatamta bivsareinu, ve'al toratcha shelimadetanu, ve'al chukeicha she'hoda'atanu, ve'al chayim chen va'chesed she'chonantanu, ve'al achilat mazon she'ata zan u'mefarnes otanu tamid be'chol yom u'vechol et u've'chol sha'a.

וְעַל הַכֹּל, יְיָ אֱלֹהֵינוּ, אֲנַחְנוּ מוֹדִים לָךְ וּמְבָרְכִים אוֹתָךְ. יִתְבָּרַךְ שִׁמְךָ בְּפִי כָּל חַי תָּמִיד לְעוֹלָם וָעֶד, כַּכָּתוּב: וְאָכַלְתָּ וְשָׂבָעְתָּ, וּבֵרַכְתָּ אֶת יְיָ אֱלֹהֶיךָ עַל הָאָרֶץ הַטּוֹבָה אֲשֶׁר נָתַן לָךְ. בָּרוּךְ אַתָּה יְיָ, עַל הָאָרֶץ וְעַל הַמָּזוֹן.

For all these things, Lord our God, we thank You. We bless Your name forever as it is written: "You have eaten and have been satisfied, and you shall bless the Lord your God for the good land that He has given you. Blessed are you, oh Lord for both the land and the food.

Ve'al hakol, Adonay eloheinu, anachnu modim lach u'mevarchim otach. Yitbarach shimcha befi kol chay tamid le'olam va'ed, kakatuv: ve'achalta ve'savata, u'verachta et Adonay eloheicha al ha'aretz ha'tova asher natan lach. Baruch ata Adonay al ha'aretz ve'al ha'mazon.

רַחֵ־ם נָא יְיָ אֱלֹהֵינוּ, עַל יִשְׂרָאֵל עַמֶּךָ, וְעַל יְרוּשָׁלַיִם עִירֶךָ, וְעַל צִיּוֹן מִשְׁכַּן כְּבוֹדֶךָ, וְעַל מַלְכוּת בֵּית דָּוִד מְשִׁיחֶךָ, וְעַל הַבַּיִת הַגָּדוֹל וְהַקָּדוֹשׁ שֶׁנִּקְרָא שִׁמְךָ עָלָיו. אֱלֹהֵינוּ, אָבִינוּ, רְעֵנוּ, זוּנֵנוּ, פַּרְנְסֵנוּ וְכַלְכְּלֵנוּ וְהַרְוִיחֵנוּ, וְהַרְוַח לָנוּ, יְיָ אֱלֹהֵינוּ, מְהֵרָה מִכָּל צָרוֹתֵינוּ וְנָא אַל תַּצְרִיכֵנוּ, יְיָ אֱלֹהֵינוּ, לֹא לִידֵי מַתְּנַת בָּשָׂר וָדָם, וְלֹא לִידֵי הַלְוָאָתָם, כִּי אִם לְיָדְךָ הַמְּלֵאָה, הַפְּתוּחָה, הַקְּדוֹשָׁה וְהָרְחָבָה, שֶׁלֹּא נֵבוֹשׁ וְלֹא נִכָּלֵם לְעוֹלָם וָעֶד.

בשבת מוסיפים

רְצֵה וְהַחֲלִיצֵנוּ, יְיָ אֱלֹהֵינוּ, בְּמִצְוֹתֶיךָ וּבְמִצְוַת יוֹם הַשְּׁבִיעִי, הַשַּׁבָּת הַגָּדוֹל וְהַקָּדוֹשׁ הַזֶּה, כִּי יוֹם זֶה גָּדוֹל וְקָדוֹשׁ הוּא לְפָנֶיךָ, לִשְׁבָּת בּוֹ וְלָנוּחַ בּוֹ בְּאַהֲבָה כְּמִצְוַת רְצוֹנֶךָ, וּבִרְצוֹנְךָ הָנִיחַ לָנוּ, יְיָ אֱלֹהֵינוּ, שֶׁלֹּא תְהֵא צָרָה וְיָגוֹן וַאֲנָחָה בְּיוֹם מְנוּחָתֵנוּ. וְהַרְאֵנוּ, יְיָ אֱלֹהֵינוּ, בְּנֶחָמַת צִיּוֹן עִירֶךָ, וּבְבִנְיַן יְרוּשָׁלַיִם עִיר קָדְשֶׁךָ, כִּי אַתָּה הוּא בַּעַל הַיְשׁוּעוֹת וּבַעַל הַנֶּחָמוֹת.

Have compassion, Lord our God, on our people Israel, and on Jerusalem, Your city, and on Zion, Your honored abode, and on the holy Temple which bears Your name. Our Father and protector, who provides us with sustenance and support, help us find relief from our woes. Let us not rely on the capriciousness of man, but upon Your open, generous giving, so that we may never bow our heads in shame and disgrace in the world to come.

(On sabbath add the following paragraph):
May You strengthen us with all your commandments, especially the commandment of making the seventh day a holy day. For You have ordained that this day is a great day on which we shall do no work, but rest from our labors. May You grant freedom from trouble or strife on this day. And may we be privileged to see Zion rebuilt in our day. For You are master of all salvation.

Rachem na Adonay Eloheinu, al Israel amecha, ve'al Yerushalayim irecha, ve'al zion mishkan kevodcha, ve'al malchut beit David meshichecha, ve'al ha'bayit ha'gadol ve'ha'kadosh shenikra shimcha alav. Eloheinu, avinu, reenu, zunenu, parnesenu ve'chalkelenu ve'harvichenu, ve'harvach lanu, Adonay Eloheinu, mehera mikol tzaroteinu. ve'na al tatzrichenu, Adonay Eloheinu, lo lydey matnat basar va'dam ve'lo lydey halvatam, ki im le'yadcha hamelea, hapetucha ha'kedosha ve'harechava, shelo nevosh ve'lo nikalem le'olam va'ed.

(On shabbat only) Retze ve'hachlitzenu, Adonay Eloheinu, bemitzvotecha u'vemitzvat yom ha'shevii, ha'shabat ha'gadol ve'ha'kadosh haze, ki ze yom gadol ve'kadosh hu lefanecha, lishbot bo ve'lanuach bo be'ahava kemitzvat retzonecha, u'virtzoncha haniach lanu Adonay Eloheinu, shelo tehe tzara ve'yagon va'anacha beyom menuchateinu. Ve'harenu, Adonay Eloheinu, benechamat Zion irecha, u'vevinyan Yerushalayim ir kodshecha, ki ata hu baal ha'yeshu'ot u'vaal ha'nechamot.

אֱלֹהֵינוּ וֵאלֹהֵי אֲבוֹתֵינוּ, יַעֲלֶה וְיָבֹא וְיַגִּיעַ, וְיֵרָאֶה וְיֵרָצֶה וְיִשָּׁמַע, וְיִפָּקֵד וְיִזָּכֵר זִכְרוֹנֵנוּ וּפִקְדוֹנֵנוּ, וְזִכְרוֹן אֲבוֹתֵינוּ, וְזִכְרוֹן מָשִׁיחַ בֶּן דָּוִד עַבְדֶּךָ, וְזִכְרוֹן יְרוּשָׁלַיִם עִיר קָדְשֶׁךָ, וְזִכְרוֹן כָּל עַמְּךָ בֵּית יִשְׂרָאֵל, לְפָנֶיךָ, לִפְלֵיטָה, לְטוֹבָה, לְחֵן וּלְחֶסֶד וּלְרַחֲמִים, לְחַיִּים וּלְשָׁלוֹם, בְּיוֹם חַג הַמַּצּוֹת הַזֶּה. זָכְרֵנוּ, יְיָ אֱלֹהֵינוּ, בּוֹ לְטוֹבָה, וּפָקְדֵנוּ בוֹ לִבְרָכָה, וְהוֹשִׁיעֵנוּ בוֹ לְחַיִּים, וּבִדְבַר יְשׁוּעָה וְרַחֲמִים חוּס וְחָנֵּנוּ, וְרַחֵם עָלֵינוּ וְהוֹשִׁיעֵנוּ, כִּי אֵלֶיךָ עֵינֵינוּ, כִּי אֵל חַנּוּן וְרַחוּם אָתָּה.

וּבְנֵה יְרוּשָׁלַיִם עִיר הַקֹּדֶשׁ בִּמְהֵרָה בְיָמֵינוּ. בָּרוּךְ אַתָּה יְיָ בּוֹנֶה בְרַחֲמָיו יְרוּשָׁלָיִם, אָמֵן.

Our God and God of our fathers, may You remember us, and may it be Your will to remember our fathers, and Jerusalem, Your city, and Your annointed servant, son of David, and all the people of Israel. Let them come to be heard and accepted by You.

May You, in Your great compassion, grant them life and peace on this feast of Matzot. Remember us on this holy day, Lord, and save us with word of grace and salvation, for we look to You as our righteous and gracious God and King.

MAY YOU BUILD UP JERUSALEM QUICKLY, IN OUR DAY. BLESSED ARE YOU, COMPASSIONATE BUILDER OF JERUSALEM, AMEN.

Eloheinu ve'elohei avoteinu, ya'ale ve'yavo ve'yagia, ve'yerae, ve'yeratze ve'yishama, ve'yipaked ve'yizacher zichronenu u'bikdonenu, ve'zichron avoteinu ve'zichron mashiach ben David avdecha, ve'zichron Yerushalayim ir kodshecha, ve'zichron kol amcha beit Israel, lefanecha, libleta, letova, lechen u'lechesed u'lerachamim, lechayim u'leshalom, beyom chag hamatzot haze, Zochreinu Adonay Eloheinu bo le'tova, u'fakdenu bo livracha ve'hoshienu bo lechayim u'vidvar yeshua, ve'rachamim chus ve'chanenu, ve'rachem aleinu ve'hoshienu, ki eleicha eineinu ki el chanun ve'rachum ata.

U'vene Yerushalayim ir hakodesh bim'hera be'yameinu. Baruch ata adonay bone berachamav yerushalayim, amen.

בָּרוּךְ אַתָּה יְיָ אֱלֹהֵינוּ מֶלֶךְ הָעוֹלָם, הָאֵל אָבִינוּ, מַלְכֵּנוּ, אַדִירֵנוּ, בּוֹרְאֵינוּ, גּוֹאֲלֵנוּ, יוֹצְרֵנוּ, קְדוֹשֵׁנוּ, קְדוֹשׁ יַעֲקֹב, רוֹעֵנוּ רוֹעֵה יִשְׂרָאֵל, הַמֶּלֶךְ הַטּוֹב וְהַמֵּטִיב לַכֹּל, שֶׁבְּכָל יוֹם וָיוֹם הוּא הֵטִיב, הוּא מֵטִיב, הוּא יֵיטִיב לָנוּ, הוּא גְמָלָנוּ, הוּא גוֹמְלֵנוּ, הוּא יִגְמְלֵנוּ לָעַד, לְחֵן וּלְחֶסֶד וּלְרַחֲמִים וּלְרֶוַח, הַצָּלָה וְהַצְלָחָה, בְּרָכָה וִישׁוּעָה, נֶחָמָה, פַּרְנָסָה וְכַלְכָּלָה, וְרַחֲמִים, וְחַיִּים וְשָׁלוֹם, וְכָל טוֹב, וּמִכָּל טוּב לְעוֹלָם אַל יְחַסְּרֵנוּ.

Blessed are You, Lord our God, King of the Universe. Our Father, our King, our Sovereign, our Creator and our Redeemer. The Holy One of Jacob, Shepherd of Israel. Great and wonderful King who daily does good to His people and will continue to do so. He bestows on us His grace forever, lavishing mercy and compassion upon us, giving us comfort and sustenance and support, commiseration and life, and peace, and all that is good. Yea, of all that is good he will never let us be in want.

Baruch ata Adonay Eloheinu melech ha'olam, ha'el avinu, malkenu, adirenu, boreinu, goaleinu, yotzrenu, kedoshenu, kedosh Yaacov, roenu roee Israel, ha'melech ha'tov ve'hameytiv lakol, shebechol yom va'yom hu heitiv, hu meitiv, hu yetiv lanu, hu gemalanu, hu gomlenu, hu yigmelenu laad, lechen u'lechesed u'lerachamim, vle'revach, hatzala, ve'hatzlach, beracha, vyshua, nechama parnasa vekalkala. Ve'rachamim ve'chayim ve'shalom ve'kol tov, u'mikol tuv le'olam al yachserenu.

הָרַחֲמָן הוּא יִמְלֹךְ עָלֵינוּ לְעוֹלָם וָעֶד.
הָרַחֲמָן הוּא יִתְבָּרַךְ בַּשָּׁמַיִם וּבָאָרֶץ.
הָרַחֲמָן הוּא יִשְׁתַּבַּח לְדוֹר דּוֹרִים, וְיִתְפָּאַר בָּנוּ לָנֶצַח נְצָחִים, וְיִתְהַדַּר בָּנוּ לָעַד וּלְעוֹלְמֵי עוֹלָמִים.
הָרַחֲמָן הוּא יְפַרְנְסֵנוּ בְּכָבוֹד.
הָרַחֲמָן הוּא יִשְׁבֹּר עֻלֵּנוּ מֵעַל צַוָּארֵנוּ וְהוּא יוֹלִיכֵנוּ קוֹמְמִיּוּת לְאַרְצֵנוּ.
הָרַחֲמָן הוּא יִשְׁלַח לָנוּ בְּרָכָה מְרֻבָּה בַּבַּיִת הַזֶּה וְעַל שֻׁלְחָן זֶה שֶׁאָכַלְנוּ עָלָיו.
הָרַחֲמָן הוּא יִשְׁלַח לָנוּ אֶת אֵלִיָּהוּ הַנָּבִיא זָכוּר לַטּוֹב וִיבַשֶּׂר לָנוּ בְּשׂוֹרוֹת טוֹבוֹת, יְשׁוּעוֹת וְנֶחָמוֹת.
הָרַחֲמָן הוּא יְבָרֵךְ אוֹתִי וְאֶת אִשְׁתִּי וְאֶת זַרְעִי וְאֶת כָּל אֲשֶׁר לִי.
הָרַחֲמָן הוּא יְבָרֵךְ אֶת אָבִי מוֹרִי בַּעַל הַבַּיִת הַזֶּה וְאֶת אִמִּי מוֹרָתִי בַּעֲלַת הַבַּיִת הַזֶּה אוֹתָנוּ וְאֶת כָּל אֲשֶׁר לָנוּ כְּמוֹ שֶׁנִּתְבָּרְכוּ אֲבוֹתֵינוּ אַבְרָהָם יִצְחָק וְיַעֲקֹב בַּכֹּל מִכֹּל כֹּל כֵּן יְבָרֵךְ אוֹתָנוּ כֻּלָּנוּ יַחַד בִּבְרָכָה שְׁלֵמָה וְנֹאמַר אָמֵן.
בַּמָּרוֹם יְלַמְּדוּ עֲלֵיהֶם וְעָלֵינוּ זְכוּת שֶׁתְּהֵא לְמִשְׁמֶרֶת שָׁלוֹם וְנִשָּׂא בְרָכָה מֵאֵת יְיָ וּצְדָקָה מֵאֱלֹהֵי יִשְׁעֵנוּ וְנִמְצָא חֵן וְשֵׂכֶל טוֹב בְּעֵינֵי אֱלֹהִים וְאָדָם.

The Merciful One shall be praised in His throne of glory. The Merciful One shall be praised in the heavens and the earth. The Merciful One shall reign over us forever. The Merciful One shall be glorified forever and ever. The Merciful One shall provide us with an honorable livelihood, one without shame, in ease and not in strife. The Merciful One shallgrant peace among us. The Merciful One shall bless all ourdoings. The Merciful One shall show us the way to succeed in our endeavors. The Merciful One shall break the yoke of exile from us and lead us forth with to our land. The Merciful One shall heal us and make us whole. The Merciful One shall open His hand to us. The Merciful One shall bless each of us in His great name as He blessed our fathers Abraham, Isaac and Jacob. In all things will the Merciful One bless us in an all-encompassing holy blessing, and let us all say: Amen. The Merciful One will spread over us His mantle of peace. The Merciful One will instill love of the Torah in our hearts and our awe of His holiness will lead us away from sin.

Harachaman, hu yimloch aleinu le'olam va'ed. Harachaman, hu yitbarach ba'shamayim u'va'aretz. Harachaman, hu yishtabach ledor dorim, ve'yitpaar banu lenetzach netzachim, ve'yithadar banu la'ad u'leolmei olamim. Harachaman, hu yefarnesenu bakavod. Harachaman, hu yishbor ulenu me'al tzavarenu ve'hu yolichenu komemiyut le'artzenu. Harachaman, hu yishlach lanu beracha meruba babayit ha'ze ve'al shulchan ze she'achalnu alav. Harachaman, hu yishlach lanu et eliyahu ha'navi zachur latov vyevaser lanu besorot tovot, yeshu'ot ve'nechamot. Harachaman, hu yevarech oti ve'et ishti ve'et zari ve'et chol asher li. Harachaman, hu yevarech et avi mori baal ha'bayit ha'ze ve'et imi morati baalat ha'bayit haze, otanu ve'et kol asher lanu, kemo shenitbarchu avoteinu Avraham, Yitzchak ve'yaacov, bakol mikol kol ken yevarech otanu kulanu yachad bivracha shlema ve'nemar amen. Bamarom yelamdu aleihem ve'aleinu zechut, shetehe lemishmeret shalom, ve'nisa beracha me'et Adonay u'tzedaka me'elohei yish'o, ve'nimtza chen ve'sechel tov be'einei elohim ve'adam.

בשבת מוסיפים
הָרַחֲמָן הוּא יַנְחִילֵנוּ יוֹם שֶׁכֻּלּוֹ שַׁבָּת וּמְנוּחָה לְחַיֵּי הָעוֹלָמִים
הָרַחֲמָן הוּא יַנְחִילֵנוּ יוֹם שֶׁכֻּלּוֹ טוֹב
הָרַחֲמָן הוּא יְזַכֵּנוּ לִימוֹת הַמָּשִׁיחַ וּלְחַיֵּי הָעוֹלָם הַבָּא
מִגְדּוֹל יְשׁוּעוֹת מַלְכּוֹ וְעֹשֶׂה חֶסֶד לִמְשִׁיחוֹ לְדָוִד וּלְזַרְעוֹ עַד עוֹלָם
עֹשֶׂה שָׁלוֹם בִּמְרוֹמָיו הוּא יַעֲשֶׂה שָׁלוֹם עָלֵינוּ וְעַל כָּל יִשְׂרָאֵל

וְאִמְרוּ אָמֵן

יְראוּ אֶת יְיָ קְדֹשָׁיו כִּי אֵין מַחְסוֹר לִירֵאָיו. כְּפִירִים רָשׁוּ וְרָעֵבוּ וְדֹרְשֵׁי יְיָ לֹא יַחְסְרוּ כָל טוֹב

הוֹדוּ לַייָ כִּי טוֹב כִּי לְעוֹלָם חַסְדּוֹ

פּוֹתֵחַ אֶת יָדֶךָ וּמַשְׂבִּיעַ לְכָל חַי רָצוֹן. בָּרוּךְ הַגֶּבֶר אֲשֶׁר יִבְטַח בַּייָ וְהָיָה יְיָ מִבְטַחוֹ
נַעַר הָיִיתִי גַם זָקַנְתִּי וְלֹא רָאִיתִי צַדִּיק נֶעֱזָב וְזַרְעוֹ מְבַקֶּשׁ לָחֶם

יְיָ עֹז לְעַמּוֹ יִתֵּן יְיָ יְבָרֵךְ אֶת עַמּוֹ בַשָּׁלוֹם

הנני מוכן ומזומן לקיים מצות כוס שלישי של ארבע כוסות לשם יחוד קודשא בריך הוא ושכינתיה
על ידי ההוא טמיר ונעלם בשם כל ישראל

בָּרוּךְ אַתָּה יְיָ אֱלֹהֵינוּ מֶלֶךְ הָעוֹלָם בּוֹרֵא פְּרִי הַגָּפֶן

שותים בהסבת שמאל

On the Sabbath, add the following: The Merciful One will grant us an eternal Sabbath day, a day of rest, after this life. The Merciful One will grant us life and bring upon us the days of the Messiah and the building of the Temple and eternal life in the world to come. The Lord is a tower of strength and salvation. He grants grace to His chosen king and shows kindness to His annointed prince, to David and His descendants forever. Though lions may starve, those who seek the Lord's grace will not lack sustenance. I was young and now I am old, and I have never seen a righteous man forsaken, nor his children lacking bread to eat. We have eaten and are satisfied, and what we have drunken, may it be to our good health. What we have left, may it be for blessing. As it is written: Blessed are you by the Lord, Creator of the heavens and the earth. Blessed is the man who trusts in the Lord, for the Lord grants strength to His people, and the Lord blesses His people with peace. (Blessing over the third cup of wine which is to be drunk while reclining):

BLESSED ARE YOU, LORD OUR GOD, WHO CREATED THE FRUIT OF THE WINE

(On Shabbat only:) Harachaman, hu yanchilenu yom shekulo shabat u'menucha lechayei ha'olamim. Harachaman, hu yanchilenu yom shekulo tov. Harachaman, hu yezakenu lymot ha'mashiach u'lechayei haolam haba. Migdol yeshu'ot malko ve'ose chesed li'meshicho le'David u'lezaro ad olam. Ose shalom bimromav, hu ya'ase shalom aleinu, ve'al kol Israel, ve'imru amen.
Yiruu et Adonay kedoshav, ki ein machsor lyre'av. Kefirim rashu ve'ra'evu ve'dorshei Adonay lo Yachseru chol tuv.

Hodu la'Adonay ki tov ki le'olam chasdo. Pote'ach et yadecha u'masbia le'chol chay ratzon. Baruch ha'gever asher yivtach ba'Adonay, ve'haya Adonay mivtacho. Naar hayiti gam zakanti ve'lo raiti tzadik ne'ezav, ve'zaro mevakesh lachem.

Adonay oz le'amo yiten Adonai yevarech et amo va'shalom.

Hineni muchan u'mezuman le'kayem mitzvat kos shelishi shel arba kosot, leshem yichud Kudsha Brich Hu u'shechintei al yedei ha'hu tamir ve'neelam beshem kol Israel. Baruch ata Adonay eloheinu melech ha'olam bore peri ha'gafen.

מוזגים כוסו של אליהו,
פותחים את הדלת ועומדים
ואומרים:

Fill the cup of Elijah the Prophet. Open the door
All rise.

אֶל־הַגּוֹיִם אֲשֶׁר לֹא יְדָעוּךָ וְעַל־מַמְלָכוֹת אֲשֶׁר בְּשִׁמְךָ לֹא קָרָאוּ: כִּי אָכַל אֶת־יַעֲקֹב וְאֶת־נָוֵהוּ הֵשַׁמּוּ: שְׁפֹךְ־עֲלֵיהֶם זַעְמֶךָ וַחֲרוֹן אַפְּךָ יַשִּׂיגֵם: תִּרְדֹּף בְּאַף וְתַשְׁמִידֵם מִתַּחַת שְׁמֵי יְיָ:

Unleash Thy wrath on the nations that reject You, and on Kingdoms that do not call Your name. For they have devoured Jacob and laid waste his dwelling place. Pursue them in fury and destroy them from under the heavens of the Lord.

סוגרים את הדלת ויושבים

Close the door and all are seated.

Shfoch chamatcha el ha'goin asher lo yeda'ucha ve'al mamlachot asher beshimcha lo kara'u: ki achal et Ya'acov ve'et navehu heshamu: shefoch aleihem za'amcha va'charon apcha yasigem: tirdof be'af ve'tashmidem mitachat shemei Adonay.

מוזגים כוס רביעי וגומרים עליו את ההלל.   Fill the Fourth cup of wine and say:

לֹא לָנוּ יְיָ לֹא לָנוּ כִּי לְשִׁמְךָ תֵּן כָּבוֹד עַל חַסְדְּךָ עַל אֲמִתֶּךָ.
לָמָּה יֹאמְרוּ הַגּוֹיִם: אַיֵּה נָא אֱלֹהֵיהֶם. וֵאלֹהֵינוּ בַשָּׁמַיִם, כֹּל אֲשֶׁר חָפֵץ עָשָׂה.
עֲצַבֵּיהֶם כֶּסֶף וְזָהָב, מַעֲשֵׂה יְדֵי אָדָם.
פֶּה לָהֶם וְלֹא יְדַבֵּרוּ, עֵינַיִם לָהֶם וְלֹא יִרְאוּ, אָזְנַיִם לָהֶם וְלֹא יִשְׁמָעוּ,
אַף לָהֶם וְלֹא יְרִיחוּן, יְדֵיהֶם וְלֹא יְמִישׁוּן, רַגְלֵיהֶם וְלֹא יְהַלֵּכוּ.
לֹא יֶהְגּוּ בִּגְרוֹנָם. כְּמוֹהֶם יִהְיוּ עֹשֵׂיהֶם. כֹּל אֲשֶׁר בֹּטֵחַ בָּהֶם.
יִשְׂרָאֵל, בְּטַח בַּיְיָ, עֶזְרָם וּמָגִנָּם הוּא.
בֵּית אַהֲרֹן בִּטְחוּ בַיְיָ, עֶזְרָם וּמָגִנָּם הוּא.
יִרְאֵי יְיָ בִּטְחוּ בַיְיָ, עֶזְרָם וּמָגִנָּם הוּא.

HALLEL
Not for us, but for the sake of Your holy name send down Your glory and Your truth. Let the nations not deride us, saying: "Where is He, this God of theirs!" Our God is in the heavens and can do all that He desires. Man-made Idols of silver and gold have mouths but they cannot speak; they have eyes but they cannot see; ears but they cannot hear; a nose, but they cannot smell. They have hands, but cannot use them; feet but they cannot walk; nor can a sound emanate from their throats; they are mute. They who make them shall become like them! Israel, trust in the Lord; He is their help and their shield. All those who revere the Lord, House oh Aron trust in the Lord; He is their help and shield.

HALEL
Lo lanu Adonay lo lanu ki leshimcha ten kavod al chasdecha al amitecha. Lama yomru ha'goyim: ayeh na eloheihem. vei'loheinu vashamayim, kol asher chafetz asa. Atzabeihem kesef ve'zahav, ma'ase yedei adam Pe lahem ve'lo yedaberu, eynayim lahem ve'lo yir'u, oznayim lahem ve'lo yishmauu, af lahem ve'lo yerichun. Yedeihem ve'lo yemishun, ragleihem ve'lo ye'halechu lo yehegu bigronam. Kemohem yihiyu oseihem. kol asher boteach bahem. Israel, betach ba'Adonay, ezram u'maginam hu: beit Aharon bitchu ba'Adonay, ezram u'maginam hu: yir'ei Adonay bitchu ba'Adonay, ezram u'maginam hu:

יְיָ זְכָרָנוּ יְבָרֵךְ. יְבָרֵךְ אֶת בֵּית יִשְׂרָאֵל, יְבָרֵךְ אֶת בֵּית אַהֲרֹן, יְבָרֵךְ יִרְאֵי יְיָ הַקְּטַנִּים עִם הַגְּדֹלִים. יֹסֵף יְיָ עֲלֵיכֶם, וְעַל בְּנֵיכֶם. בְּרוּכִים אַתֶּם לַיְיָ, עֹשֵׂה שָׁמַיִם וָאָרֶץ. הַשָּׁמַיִם שָׁמַיִם לַיְיָ, וְהָאָרֶץ נָתַן לִבְנֵי אָדָם. לֹא הַמֵּתִים יְהַלְלוּ יָהּ, וְלֹא כָּל יֹרְדֵי דוּמָה. וַאֲנַחְנוּ נְבָרֵךְ יָהּ, מֵעַתָּה וְעַד עוֹלָם, הַלְלוּיָהּ.

The Lord who has remembered us will bless us and the house of Israel and the house of Aaron. He will bless the great and the small. May the Lord grant you and your children prosperity. You are blessed of the Lord, Who has made the heavens and the earth. The heavens are the Lord's, but the earth He has given to mankind. The dead cannot praise the Lord, nor can they who descend in to silence. But we shall bless the Lord from now and forever, Halleluyah.

Adonay zecharanu yevarech Yevarech et beit Israel, yevarech et beit Aharon, yevarech yirei Adonay ha'ketanim im ha'gedolim. Yosef Adonay aleichem, aleichem ve'al beneichem. Beruchim atem la'Adonay, ose shamayim va'aretz. Ha'shamayim shamayim la'Adonay, ve'ha'aretz natan livnei adam. Lo ha'metim yehalelu Ya, ve'lo kol yordei duma. Va'anachnu nevarech Ya, me'ata ve'ad olam, haleluya.

כִּי יִשְׁמַע יְיָ אֶת קוֹלִי תַּחֲנוּנָי. כִּי הִטָּה אָזְנוֹ לִי וּבְיָמַי אֶקְרָא. אֲפָפוּנִי חֶבְלֵי מָוֶת וּמְצָרֵי שְׁאוֹל מְצָאוּנִי. צָרָה וְיָגוֹן אֶמְצָא וּבְשֵׁם יְיָ אֶקְרָא. אָנָּא יְיָ מַלְּטָה נַפְשִׁי. חַנּוּן יְיָ וְצַדִּיק וֵאלֹהֵינוּ מְרַחֵם. שֹׁמֵר פְּתָאִים יְיָ, דַּלּוֹתִי וְלִי יְהוֹשִׁיעַ. שׁוּבִי נַפְשִׁי לִמְנוּחָיְכִי כִּי יְיָ גָּמַל עָלָיְכִי כִּי חִלַּצְתָּ נַפְשִׁי מִמָּוֶת, אֶת עֵינִי מִן דִּמְעָה, אֶת רַגְלִי מִדֶּחִי. אֶתְהַלֵּךְ לִפְנֵי יְיָ בְּאַרְצוֹת הַחַיִּים. הֶאֱמַנְתִּי כִּי אֲדַבֵּר אֲנִי עָנִיתִי מְאֹד. אֲנִי אָמַרְתִּי בְחָפְזִי כָּל הָאָדָם כֹּזֵב.

(Psalm 116:1-11) I love that the Lord hears my voice in supplication. For He has bent His ear to me, and I shall call out to Him all my days. Though the strands of death have wrapped themselves upon me; the pains of the grave have overtaken me, and I was filled with trouble and sorrow; then I called out to the Lord; Lord, save me. Gracious is he, and merciful. The Lord protects the innocent. I was low and He saved me. Rest, my soul, for the Lord has been kind to you. You have delivered my soul from death, my eyes from tears, and my feet from stumbling. I shall walk before the Lord in the land of the living. I have kept faith even when sorely afflicted, and even when I have said: "All men are deceitful."

Ahavti ki yishma Adonay et koli tachanunai. Ki hita ozno li, u'veyamay ekra. Afafuni chevley mavet, u'metzarei sheol metzauni, tzara ve'yagon emtza u'veshem Adonay ekra. Ana Adonay malta nafshi. Chanun Adonay ve'tzadik veieloheinu merachem. Shomer petaim Adonay, daloti ve'li yehoshia. Shuvi nafshi limenuchaychi ki Adonay gamal alaychi ki chilatzta nafshi mimavet, et eini min dimaa, et ragli midechi. Ethalech lifnei Adonay be'artzot ha'chayim. He'emanti ki adaber, ani anite meod. Ani amarti be'chofzi kol ha'adam kozev.

מָה אָשִׁיב לַי־

כׇּל־תַּגְמוּלוֹהִי עָלָי. כּוֹס יְשׁוּעוֹת אֶשָּׂא וּבְשֵׁם יְיָ אֶקְרָא. נְדָרַי לַיְיָ אֲשַׁלֵּם נֶגְדָה־נָּא לְכׇל־עַמּוֹ. יָקָר בְּעֵינֵי יְיָ הַמָּוְתָה לַחֲסִידָיו. אָנָּה יְיָ כִּי־אֲנִי עַבְדֶּךָ, אֲנִי־עַבְדְּךָ בֶּן־אֲמָתֶךָ פִּתַּחְתָּ לְמוֹסֵרָי. לְךָ־אֶזְבַּח זֶבַח תּוֹדָה וּבְשֵׁם יְיָ אֶקְרָא. נְדָרַי לַיְיָ אֲשַׁלֵּם נֶגְדָה־נָּא לְכׇל־עַמּוֹ. בְּחַצְרוֹת בֵּית יְיָ בְּתוֹכֵכִי יְרוּשָׁלָֽיִם הַלְלוּיָהּ

How can I repay the Lord for His kindness to me? I shall raise the cup of salvation and call out the name of the Lord. My oaths to the Lord I will fulfill in the presence of all His people. Grievous in the Lord's sight is the death of His pious believers. Please, Lord, I am truly Your servant, Your bondsman, the son of Your handmaiden. You have loosened my bonds. To You I offer a thanksgiving sacrifice, and call upon the name of the Lord. My oaths to the Lord I shall fulfill in the presence of all His people, in the courts of the Lord's house, in the midst of Jerusalem. Halleluyah.

Ma ashiv la'adonay kol tagmulohi alay, kos yeshu'ot esa u'veshem adonay ekra. Nedaray la'adonay ashalem, negda na le'chol amo. Yakar be'einei adonay hamavta la'chasidav. Anaadonay ki ani avdecha, ani avdecha ben amatecha pitachta lemosray. Lecha ezbach zevach toda u'veshem adonay ekra. Nedarai la'adonay ashalem, negda na lechol amo. Be'chatzerot beit adonay, be'tochechi Yerushalayim. Halleluyah.

הַלְלוּ אֶת־יְיָ כׇּל־גּוֹיִם שַׁבְּחוּהוּ כׇּל־הָאֻמִּים כִּי גָבַר עָלֵינוּ חַסְדּוֹ וֶאֱמֶת־יְיָ לְעוֹלָם הַלְלוּיָהּ

Give thanks to the Lord, all the nations; praise Him, all the peoples! For His lovingkindness is immense and overwhelming, and the Lord's truth lasts forever, halleluyah!

Halelu et Adonay kol goyim shabchuhu kol ha'umim ki gavar aleinu chasdo ve'emet Adonay le'olam Haleluya.

הוֹדוּ לַיְיָ כִּי טוֹב
יֹאמַר נָא יִשְׂרָאֵל
יֹאמְרוּ נָא בֵית אַהֲרֹן
יֹאמְרוּ נָא יִרְאֵי יְיָ

Give thanks to the Lord for He is good; His kindness endures forever. Let Israel say: His kindness endures forever Let the House of Aaron say: His kindness endures forever Let those who revere the Lord say: His kindness endures forever.

Hodu la'Adonai ki tov. Ki le'olam chasdo. Yomar na Israel. Ki le'olam chasdo. Yomro na beit Aharon. Ki le'olam chasdo. Yomru na yir'ei Adonay. Ki le'olam chasdo.

מִן הַמֵּצַר קָרָאתִי יָּהּ עָנָנִי בַמֶּרְחָב יָהּ: יְיָ לִי לֹא אִירָא: מַה יַּעֲשֶׂה לִי אָדָם: יְיָ לִי בְּעֹזְרָי וַאֲנִי אֶרְאֶה בְשֹׂנְאָי: טוֹב לַחֲסוֹת בַּייָ מִבְּטֹחַ בָּאָדָם: טוֹב לַחֲסוֹת בַּייָ מִבְּטֹחַ בִּנְדִיבִים: כָּל גּוֹיִם סְבָבוּנִי בְּשֵׁם יְיָ כִּי אֲמִילַם: סַבּוּנִי גַם סְבָבוּנִי בְּשֵׁם יְיָ כִּי אֲמִילַם: סַבּוּנִי כִדְבוֹרִים דֹּעֲכוּ כְּאֵשׁ קוֹצִים בְּשֵׁם יְיָ כִּי אֲמִילַם: דָּחֹה דְחִיתַנִי לִנְפֹּל וַייָ עֲזָרָנִי: עָזִּי וְזִמְרָת יָהּ וַיְהִי לִי לִישׁוּעָה: קוֹל רִנָּה וִישׁוּעָה בְּאָהֳלֵי צַדִּיקִים: יְמִין יְיָ עֹשָׂה חָיִל: יְמִין יְיָ רוֹמֵמָה. יְמִין יְיָ עֹשָׂה חָיִל: לֹא אָמוּת כִּי אֶחְיֶה וַאֲסַפֵּר מַעֲשֵׂי יָהּ: יַסֹּר יִסְּרַנִּי יָּהּ וְלַמָּוֶת לֹא נְתָנָנִי: פִּתְחוּ לִי שַׁעֲרֵי צֶדֶק אָבֹא בָם אוֹדֶה יָהּ: זֶה הַשַּׁעַר לַייָ צַדִּיקִים יָבֹאוּ בוֹ:

From narrow straits I called out unto the Lord, and the Lord answered me by placing me in a wide expanse. The Lord is with me; I do not fear what mankind may do to me. The Lord is with me and with my helpers, and I shall see my enemies defeated. It is better to trust the Lord than man; it is better to trust the Lord than noble princes. All nations have surrounded me, but in the name of the Lord I have chased them off. They whirled around me, but in the name of the Lord I cut them down. They swarmed like bees about me, but they were extinguished like thorns put to the flame. In the name of the Lord I cut them down. Men pushed against me that I might fall, but the Lord helped me. The Lord is my strength and my salvation. The sound of rejoicing and salvation can be heard in the tents of the righteous. The Lord's right hand does valiantly, it is raised in triumph. The Lord's right hand does valiantly. I shall not die, but live to tell of the deeds of the Lord. The Lord has sometimes punished me, but He has not left me to die. Open for me the gates of righteousness, that I may enter and praise the Lord. This is the gate of the Lord, the righteous may enter through it.

Min ha'meytzar karati Ya anani ba'merchav Ya: Adonay li lo ira: ma yaase li adam: Adonay li beozray va'ani er'e be'sonai: tov lachasot ba'Adonay mibto'ach ba'adam: tov lachasot ba'Adonay mibto'ach bindivin: Kol goyim sevavuni beshem Adonay ki amilam: sabuni gam sevavuni beshem Adonay ki amilam: sabuni kidevorim do'achu ke'esh kotzim beshem Adonay ki amilam: dacho dechitani linpol va'Adonay azarani: ozi ve'zimrat Ya va'yehi li liyshua: kol rina viyshua be'oholei tzadikim: yemin Adonay osa chayil yemin Adonay romema: yemim Adonay osa chayil: lo amut ki echye va'asaper ma'asei Ya: yasor yisrani Ya ve'lamavet lo netanani: pitchu li shaarei tzedek avo vam ode Ya: ze hashaar la'Adonay tzadikim yavo'u vo:

חוזרים פעמיים על כל פסוק

אוֹדְךָ כִּי עֲנִיתָנִי וַתְּהִי לִי לִישׁוּעָה: אֶבֶן מָאֲסוּ הַבּוֹנִים הָיְתָה לְרֹאשׁ פִּנָּה: מֵאֵת יְיָ הָיְתָה זֹּאת הִיא נִפְלָאת בְּעֵינֵינוּ: זֶה הַיּוֹם עָשָׂה יְיָ נָגִילָה וְנִשְׂמְחָה בוֹ:

Each verse is said twice

I thank You, for You have answered me and become my salvation. The stone that was rejected by the builders has become the building's main cornerstone. This is the Lord's work and is marvelous in our eyes. This is the day that the Lord has made; we shall rejoice and be glad on this day.
We beseech thee' O Lord!
Save us now!
We beseech, O Lord!
Cause us to prosper now!
Blessed is he that comes in the name of the Lord. We bless you from the house of the Lord.

חוזרים פעמיים על כל פסוק

בָּרוּךְ הַבָּא בְּשֵׁם יְיָ. בֵּרַכְנוּכֶם מִבֵּית יְיָ: אֵל יְיָ וַיָּאֶר לָנוּ אִסְרוּ חַג בַּעֲבֹתִים עַד קַרְנוֹת הַמִּזְבֵּחַ: אֵלִי אַתָּה וְאוֹדֶךָּ אֱלֹהַי אֲרוֹמְמֶךָּ: הוֹדוּ לַיְיָ כִּי טוֹב כִּי לְעוֹלָם חַסְדּוֹ:

Almighty is the Lord, and he has enlightened us, the festive offering with cords to the horns of the altar! My God are thou, and I will render thanks unto thee; My God I will extol thee. Give thanks unto the Lord, for He's good His kindness endures forever.

Odcha ki anitani va'tehi li liyshu'a: even maasu ha'bonim hayta lerosh pina: me'et Adonay hayta zot hi niflat be'eineinu: ze hayom asa Adonay nagila ve'nismecha vo.

Ana Adonay hoshi'a na, Ana Adonay hoshi'a na Ana Adonay hatzlicha na Ana Adonay hatzlicha na

Baruch haba beshem Adonay. Berachnuchem mibeit Adonay: El Adonay va'yaer lanu isru chag ba'avotim ad karnot ha'mizbe'ach: eli ata ve'odecha. Elohay aromemecha: hodu la'Adonay ki tov ki le'olam chasdo.

הוֹדוּ לֵאלֹהֵי הָאֱלֹהִים	כִּי לְעוֹלָם חַסְדּוֹ		כִּי לְעוֹלָם חַסְדּוֹ	וַיְנַעֵר פַּרְעֹה וְחֵילוֹ בְיַם סוּף	כִּי לְעוֹלָם חַסְדּוֹ
הוֹדוּ לַאֲדֹנֵי הָאֲדֹנִים	כִּי לְעוֹלָם חַסְדּוֹ		כִּי לְעוֹלָם חַסְדּוֹ	לְמוֹלִיךְ עַמּוֹ בַּמִּדְבָּר	כִּי לְעוֹלָם חַסְדּוֹ
לְעֹשֵׂה נִפְלָאוֹת גְּדֹלוֹת לְבַדּוֹ	כִּי לְעוֹלָם חַסְדּוֹ		כִּי לְעוֹלָם חַסְדּוֹ	לְמַכֵּה מְלָכִים גְּדֹלִים	כִּי לְעוֹלָם חַסְדּוֹ
לְעֹשֵׂה הַשָּׁמַיִם בִּתְבוּנָה	כִּי לְעוֹלָם חַסְדּוֹ		כִּי לְעוֹלָם חַסְדּוֹ	וַיַּהֲרֹג מְלָכִים אַדִּירִים	כִּי לְעוֹלָם חַסְדּוֹ
לְרוֹקַע הָאָרֶץ עַל הַמָּיִם	כִּי לְעוֹלָם חַסְדּוֹ		כִּי לְעוֹלָם חַסְדּוֹ	לְסִיחוֹן מֶלֶךְ הָאֱמֹרִי	כִּי לְעוֹלָם חַסְדּוֹ
לְעֹשֵׂה אוֹרִים גְּדֹלִים	כִּי לְעוֹלָם חַסְדּוֹ		כִּי לְעוֹלָם חַסְדּוֹ	וּלְעוֹג מֶלֶךְ הַבָּשָׁן	כִּי לְעוֹלָם חַסְדּוֹ
אֶת הַשֶּׁמֶשׁ לְמֶמְשֶׁלֶת בַּיּוֹם	כִּי לְעוֹלָם חַסְדּוֹ		כִּי לְעוֹלָם חַסְדּוֹ	וְנָתַן אַרְצָם לְנַחֲלָה	כִּי לְעוֹלָם חַסְדּוֹ
אֶת הַיָּרֵחַ וְכוֹכָבִים לְמֶמְשְׁלוֹת בַּלָּיְלָה	כִּי לְעוֹלָם חַסְדּוֹ		כִּי לְעוֹלָם חַסְדּוֹ	נַחֲלָה לְיִשְׂרָאֵל עַבְדּוֹ	כִּי לְעוֹלָם חַסְדּוֹ
לְמַכֵּה מִצְרַיִם בִּבְכוֹרֵיהֶם	כִּי לְעוֹלָם חַסְדּוֹ		כִּי לְעוֹלָם חַסְדּוֹ	שֶׁבְּשִׁפְלֵנוּ זָכַר לָנוּ	כִּי לְעוֹלָם חַסְדּוֹ
וַיּוֹצֵא יִשְׂרָאֵל מִתּוֹכָם	כִּי לְעוֹלָם חַסְדּוֹ		כִּי לְעוֹלָם חַסְדּוֹ	וַיִּפְרְקֵנוּ מִצָּרֵינוּ	כִּי לְעוֹלָם חַסְדּוֹ
בְּיָד חֲזָקָה וּבִזְרוֹעַ נְטוּיָה	כִּי לְעוֹלָם חַסְדּוֹ		כִּי לְעוֹלָם חַסְדּוֹ	נֹתֵן לֶחֶם לְכָל בָּשָׂר	כִּי לְעוֹלָם חַסְדּוֹ
לְגֹזֵר יַם סוּף לִגְזָרִים	כִּי לְעוֹלָם חַסְדּוֹ		כִּי לְעוֹלָם חַסְדּוֹ	הוֹדוּ לְאֵל הַשָּׁמָיִם	כִּי לְעוֹלָם חַסְדּוֹ
וְהֶעֱבִיר יִשְׂרָאֵל בְּתוֹכוֹ	כִּי לְעוֹלָם חַסְדּוֹ				

GIVE THANKS TO THE LORD, FOR HE IS GOOD:
HIS KINDNESS ENDURES FOREVER

Give thanks to the God of Gods:	His kindness endures forever
Give thanks to the Lord of Lords:	His kindness endures forever
To Him who performs wonders:	His kindness endures forever
To Him who creates the heavens in wisdom:	His kindness endures forever
To Him who laid the earth over the waters:	His kindness endures forever
To Him who made the great lights:	His kindness endures forever
The sun to rule by day:	His kindness endures forever
The moon and stars by night:	His kindness endures forever
To Him who smote Egypt's first-born:	His kindness endures forever
And took Israel out from among them:	His kindness endures forever
With a strong hand and an outstretched arm:	His kindness endures forever
To Him who parted the Red Sea:	His kindness endures forever
And caused Israel to pass through it:	His kindness endures forever
And threw Pharaoh and his host into the Sea:	His kindness endures forever
To Him who led His people through the wilderness:	His kindness endures forever
To Him who smote great kings:	His kindness endures forever
And slew mighty rulers:	His kindness endures forever
Sihon, king of the Amorites:	His kindness endures forever
And Og, king of Bashan:	His kindness endures forever
And gave their land as an inheritance:	His kindness endures forever
An inheritance to Israel, His servant:	His kindness endures forever
He who remembered us when we were bowed low:	His kindness endures forever
And delivered us from our enemies:	His kindness endures forever
To Him who provides sustenance to all living creatures:	His kindness endures forever
Give thanks to the God of heaven:	His kindness endures forever.

Hodu La'Adonay ki tov: ki Le'olam chasdo

Hodu' le'elohei ha'elohim: ki le'olam chasdo
Hodu la'Adoney ha'adonim: ki le'olam chasdo
Leose nifla'ot gedolot levado: ki le'olam chasdo
Le'ose ha'shamayim bitevuna: ki le'olam chasdo
le'roka ha'aretz al ha'mayim: ki le'olam chasdo
le'ose orim gedolim: ki le'olam chasdo
et hashemesh lememshelet bayom: ki le'olam chasdo
et ha'yareach ve'chochavim lememshelot ba'layla: ki le'olam chasdo
lamake Mitzrayim biv'choreyhem: ki le'olam chasdo
va'yotzeh Israel mitocham: ki le'olam chasdo
beyad chazaka u'vizroa netuya: ki le'olam chasdo
le'gozer yam suf ligzarim: ki le'olam chasdo
ve'he'evir Israel betocho: ki le'olam chasdo
ve'nier Par'o ve'cheilo ve'yam suf: ki le'olam chasdo
le'molich amo bamidbar: ki le'olam chasdo
lemake melachim gedolim: ki le'olam chasdo
va'yaharog melachim adirim: ki le'olam chasdo
le'sichon melech ha'emori: ki le'olam chasdo
u'le'og melech habashan: ki le'olam chasdo
ve'natan artzam lenachala: ki le'olam chasdo
nachala le'Israel avdo: ki le'olam chasdo
she'beshiflenu zachar lanu: ki le'olam chasdo
va'yifrekenu mitzareinu: ki le'olam chasdo
noten lechem lechol basar: ki le'olam chasdo
hodu le'el hashamayim: ki le'olam chasdo.

נִשְׁמַת כָּל חַי תְּבָרֵךְ אֶת שִׁמְךָ יְיָ אֱלֹהֵינוּ וְרוּחַ כָּל בָּשָׂר תְּפָאֵר וּתְרוֹמֵם זִכְרְךָ מַלְכֵּנוּ תָּמִיד מִן הָעוֹלָם וְעַד הָעוֹלָם אַתָּה אֵל. וּמִבַּלְעָדֶיךָ אֵין לָנוּ מֶלֶךְ גּוֹאֵל וּמוֹשִׁיעַ. פּוֹדֶה וּמַצִּיל. וּמְפַרְנֵס בְּכָל עֵת צָרָה וְצוּקָה. אֵין לָנוּ מֶלֶךְ אֶלָּא אָתָּה. אֱלֹהֵי הָרִאשׁוֹנִים וְהָאַחֲרוֹנִים, אֱלוֹהַּ כָּל בְּרִיּוֹת, אֲדוֹן כָּל תּוֹלָדוֹת, הַמְהֻלָּל בְּכָל הַתִּשְׁבָּחוֹת, הַמְנַהֵג עוֹלָמוֹ בְּחֶסֶד וּבְרִיּוֹתָיו בְּרַחֲמִים. וַיְיָ לֹא יָנוּם וְלֹא יִישָׁן, הַמְעוֹרֵר יְשֵׁנִים, וְהַמֵּקִיץ נִרְדָּמִים, וְהַמֵּשִׂיחַ אִלְּמִים, וְהַמַּתִּיר אֲסוּרִים, וְהַסּוֹמֵךְ נוֹפְלִים, וְהַזּוֹקֵף כְּפוּפִים. לְךָ לְבַדְּךָ אֲנַחְנוּ מוֹדִים. אִלּוּ פִינוּ מָלֵא שִׁירָה כַּיָּם, וּלְשׁוֹנֵנוּ רִנָּה כַּהֲמוֹן גַּלָּיו, וְשִׂפְתוֹתֵינוּ — שֶׁבַח כְּמֶרְחֲבֵי רָקִיעַ, וְעֵינֵינוּ מְאִירוֹת כַּשֶּׁמֶשׁ וְכַיָּרֵחַ, וְיָדֵינוּ פְרוּשׂוֹת כְּנִשְׁרֵי שָׁמָיִם, וְרַגְלֵינוּ קַלּוֹת כָּאַיָּלוֹת, אֵין אֲנוּ מַסְפִּיקִים לְהוֹדוֹת לְךָ, יְיָ אֱלֹהֵינוּ, וֵאלֹהֵי אֲבוֹתֵינוּ וּלְבָרֵךְ אֶת שְׁמֶךָ, עַל אַחַת מֵאֶלֶף אַלְפֵי אֲלָפִים וְרֹב רִבֵּי רְבָבוֹת פְּעָמִים, הַטּוֹבוֹת שֶׁעָשִׂיתָ עִם אֲבוֹתֵינוּ וְעִמָּנוּ. מִמִּצְרַיִם גְּאַלְתָּנוּ, יְיָ אֱלֹהֵינוּ, מִבֵּית עֲבָדִים פְּדִיתָנוּ, בְּרָעָב זַנְתָּנוּ, וּבְשָׂבָע כִּלְכַּלְתָּנוּ, מֵחֶרֶב הִצַּלְתָּנוּ, מִדֶּבֶר מִלַּטְתָּנוּ, וּמֵחֳלָיִם רָעִים וְנֶאֱמָנִים דִּלִּיתָנוּ. עַד הֵנָּה עֲזָרוּנוּ רַחֲמֶיךָ, וְלֹא עֲזָבוּנוּ חֲסָדֶיךָ, וְאַל תִּטְּשֵׁנוּ יְיָ אֱלֹהֵינוּ לָנֶצַח. עַל כֵּן אֵבָרִים שֶׁפִּלַּגְתָּ בָּנוּ, וְרוּחַ וּנְשָׁמָה שֶׁנָּפַחְתָּ בְּאַפֵּינוּ, וְלָשׁוֹן אֲשֶׁר שַׂמְתָּ בְּפִינוּ — הֵן הֵם יוֹדוּ וִיבָרְכוּ, וִישַׁבְּחוּ וִיפָאֲרוּ, וִירוֹמְמוּ וְיַעֲרִיצוּ, וְיַקְדִּישׁוּ וְיַמְלִיכוּ אֶת שִׁמְךָ מַלְכֵּנוּ. כִּי כָל פֶּה לְךָ יוֹדֶה, וְכָל לָשׁוֹן לְךָ תִּשָּׁבַע, וְכָל בֶּרֶךְ לְךָ תִכְרַע, וְכָל קוֹמָה לְפָנֶיךָ תִשְׁתַּחֲוֶה, וְכָל לְבָבוֹת יִירָאוּךָ, וְכָל קֶרֶב וּכְלָיוֹת יְזַמְּרוּ לִשְׁמֶךָ. כַּדָּבָר שֶׁכָּתוּב: כָּל עַצְמוֹתַי תֹּאמַרְנָה יְיָ מִי כָמוֹךָ, מַצִּיל עָנִי מֵחָזָק מִמֶּנּוּ, וְעָנִי וְאֶבְיוֹן מִגּוֹזְלוֹ, מִי יִדְמֶה לָּךְ? וּמִי יִשְׁוֶה לָּךְ? וּמִי יַעֲרָךְ לָךְ? הָאֵל הַגָּדוֹל הַגִּבּוֹר וְהַנּוֹרָא, אֵל עֶלְיוֹן קוֹנֵה שָׁמַיִם וָאָרֶץ. נְהַלֶּלְךָ וּנְשַׁבֵּחֲךָ וּנְפָאֶרְךָ וּנְבָרֵךְ אֶת שֵׁם קָדְשֶׁךָ. כָּאָמוּר: לְדָוִד, בָּרְכִי נַפְשִׁי אֶת יְיָ, וְכָל קְרָבַי אֶת שֵׁם קָדְשׁוֹ: הָאֵל בְּתַעֲצֻמוֹת עֻזֶּךָ, הַגָּדוֹל בִּכְבוֹד שְׁמֶךָ, הַגִּבּוֹר לָנֶצַח וְהַנּוֹרָא בְּנוֹרְאוֹתֶיךָ. הַמֶּלֶךְ הַיּוֹשֵׁב עַל כִּסֵּא רָם וְנִשָּׂא. שׁוֹכֵן עַד מָרוֹם וְקָדוֹשׁ שְׁמוֹ. וְכָתוּב: רַנְּנוּ צַדִּיקִים בַּיְיָ, לַיְשָׁרִים נָאוָה תְהִלָּה, בְּפִי יְשָׁרִים תִּתְהַלָּל, וּבְדִבְרֵי צַדִּיקִים תִּתְבָּרַךְ, וּבִלְשׁוֹן חֲסִידִים תִּתְרוֹמָם, וּבְקֶרֶב קְדוֹשִׁים תִּתְקַדָּשׁ. וּבְמַקְהֲלוֹת רִבְבוֹת עַמְּךָ בֵּית יִשְׂרָאֵל, בְּרִנָּה יִתְפָּאֵר שִׁמְךָ מַלְכֵּנוּ בְּכָל דּוֹר וָדוֹר. שֶׁכֵּן חוֹבַת כָּל הַיְצוּרִים לְפָנֶיךָ, יְיָ אֱלֹהֵינוּ, וֵאלֹהֵי אֲבוֹתֵינוּ לְהוֹדוֹת, לְהַלֵּל, לְשַׁבֵּחַ, לְפָאֵר, לְרוֹמֵם, לְהַדֵּר, לְבָרֵךְ, לְעַלֵּה, וּלְקַלֵּס. עַל כָּל דִּבְרֵי שִׁירוֹת וְתִשְׁבְּחוֹת דָּוִד בֶּן יִשַׁי עַבְדְּךָ מְשִׁיחֶךָ.

The soul of all living things shall bless Your name, Eternal our God; the spirit of all flesh shall ever adore and extol Your fame, our King. From everlasting to everlasting You are God, and besides You we have no Ruler or Deliverer. Redeemer, Sustainer, Who is merciful in every time of sorrow and distress. We have no King except You. O God of the beginning and of the end. God of all creatures. Master of all existence, Who is praised in manifold praises. Who leads the world with loving and kindness and His creatures with mercy: God Who neither slumbers nor sleeps, awakens the sleeping, stirs and the slumbering, gives speech to the dumb and releases the bound, supports the falling and raises up the bowed-down. To You alone we give thanks. Were our mouths filled with singing as the sea, and our tongue uplifted in song as the waves, and our lips with praise as the spacious firmament, and our eyes shining as the sun and the moon, and our hands stretched out as the eagles of the skies, and our feet swift as the hinds we would still not be able to offer proper thanks to You, Eternal our God and God of our fathers, and to praise Your Name one thousandth share or even a tenth of one thousandth share for the manifold goodness You bestowed upon our forefathers and upon us. From Egypt You redeemed us, O Eternal our God, and from the house of bondage You liberated us. In famine You fed us, in plenty You sustained us, from the sword You saved us, from pestilence You delivered us, from severe sickness You spared us. Heretofore Your mercy helped us and Your loving kindness did not forsake us. Do not forsake us evermore, we pray You, Eternal our God. Therefore, the limbs You have fashioned within us, and the spirit of life which You have breathed into us, and the tongue which You have placed in our mouth, they shall all thank, praise, extol, glorify, exalt, adore, hallow, and give sovereignty to Your name, for every mouth shall give thanks to You, and every tongue shall pledge fealty to You; and every knee shall bend to You, and every living being shall bow down to You; all hearts shall revere You, and all beings shall sing to Your name as it is written: "All my being shall say, Eternal, who is like unto Thee, delivering the afflicted from one stronger than he, and the needy from one who would rob him!" Who is like unto You, and who can equal You? Who can compare with You, O God, great, mighty, revered, supreme God, Master of heaven and earth? Let us praise and worship, glorify and bless Your holy name, as it is said by David: "O my soul, bless the Eternal, and all that is within me. Bless His holy name." You are God by the power of Your might, great by the glory of Your Name, almighty forever and inspiring awe by Your deeds. You are the Ruler sublimely enthroned and exalted. You Who dwell in eternity, exalted and holy is Your Name. And it is written: "Rejoice in the Eternal, ye righteous, for it becometh the upright to speak His praise." By the mouth of the upright You shall be lauded, and by the words of the righteous You shall be praised: by the tongue of the pious You shall be exalted, and in the midst of the holy You shall be hallowed. In the assemblies of the multitudes of Your people the House of Israel, Your name, O our Ruler, shall be glorified with song in every generation. For it is the duty of all creatures to give thanks, to praise, to exalt, to bless, to adore and to extol You, O Eternal our God, and the God of our fathers, in the words of the songs and psalms of David the son of Jesse, Your annointed servant.

Nishmat kol chai tevarech et shimcha, Adonay Eloheinu, ve'ruach kol basar tefa'er u'teromem zichrecha malkenu tamid. Min ha'olam ve'ad ha'olam ata El u'mibaladecha ein lanu melech goel u'moshia. Podeh u'matzil u'mefarnes be'chol et tzara ve'tzuka. Ein lanu melech ela ata. Elohei ha'rishonim ve'ha'acharonim, eloha kol briyot, adon kol toladot, ha'mehulal bechol ha'tishbachot, ha'menaheg olamo bechesed u'veriyotav berachamim. Va'Adonay lo yanum ve'lo yishan, ha'meorer yeshenim, ve'hamekitz nirdamim, ve'hamesiach ilmim, ve'hamatir asurim, ve'hasomech noflim, ve'hazokef kefufim. Lecha levadcha anachnu modim. Ilu finu male shira kayam, u'leshonenu - rina kahamon galav, ve'siftoteinu - shevach kemerchavei rakia, ve'eineinu me'irot kashemesh ve'chayare'ach, ve'yadeinu prusot kenishrei shamayim, ve'ragleinu kalot ka'ayalot - ein anachnu maspikim le'hodot lecha, Adonay Eloheinu veilohey avoteinu u'levarech et shmecha, al achat me'alef elef alfei alafim ve'ribei revavot pe'amim ha'tovot she'asita im avoteinu ve'imanu. mi'Mitzrayim ge'altanu Adonay Eloheinu, mibeit avadim peditanu, beraav zantanu, u'vesova kilkaltanu, mecherev hitzaltanu, u'midever milatetanu, u'mecholayim ra'im ve'ne'emanim dilitanu. Ad hena azarunu rachamecha, ve'lo azavunu chasadecha, ve'al titshenu Adonay Eloheinu lanetzach. Al ken evarim shepilagta banu, ve'ru'ach u'neshama she'nafachta ve'apeinu ve'lashon asher samta befinu - hen-hem yodu viyvarchu, viyshabchu viyfaaru, viyromemu ve'yaaritzu, ve'yakdishu ve'yamlichu et shimcha malkenu. Ki chol peh lecha yodeh, ve'chol lashon lecha tishava, ve'chol berech lecha tichra, ve'chol koma le'fanecha tishtachaveh, ve'chol levavot yiraucha, ve'chol kerev u'chlayot yezamru li'shmecha, kadavar shekatuv: kol atzmotai tomarna: Adonay, mi chamocha, matzil ani me'chazak mimenu, ve'ani ve'evyon migozlo. Mi yidme lach? u'mi yishveh? u'mi ya'aroch lach? ha'El hagadol, hagibor ve'hanora, El Elyon koneh shamayim va'aretz. nehalelcha, u'neshabechacha, u'nefa'ercha u'nevarech et shem kodshecha, ka'amur: le'David, barchi nafshi et Adonay, ve'chol keravay et shem kodsho: ha'El be'ta'atzumot u'zecha, hagadol bichvod shmecha, higibor lanetzach ve'ha'nora benor'o'techa, Hamelech ha'yoshev al kise' ram ve'nisa. Shochen ad, marom ve'kadosh shemo, ve'chatuv: ranenu tzadikim ba'Adonay, la'yesharim nava tehila. Be'fi yesharim tithalal, u'vedivrei tzadikim titbarach, u'vileshon chasidim titromam, u'vekerev kedoshim titkadash: u'vemakhalot rivevot amcha beit Israel be'rina yitpaar shimcha, malkenu, be'chol dor va'dor, sheken chovat kol ha'yetzurim lefanecha Adonay Eloheinu veilohei avoteinu, hle'hodot, le'halel, le'shabe'ach, le'fa'er, leromem, le'hader, le'varech, le'aleh u'lekales, al kol divrei shirot ve'tishbachot David ben Yishai avdecha meshichecha:

שִׁמְךָ לָעַד מַלְכֵּנוּ, הָאֵל הַמֶּלֶךְ הַגָּדוֹל וְהַקָּדוֹשׁ בַּשָּׁמַיִם וּבָאָרֶץ, כִּי לְךָ נָאֶה יְיָ אֱלֹהֵינוּ וֵאלֹהֵי אֲבוֹתֵינוּ לְעוֹלָם וָעֶד. שִׁיר וּשְׁבָחָה, הַלֵּל וְזִמְרָה, עֹז וּמֶמְשָׁלָה, נֶצַח, גְּדֻלָּה וּגְבוּרָה, תְּהִלָּה וְתִפְאֶרֶת, קְדֻשָּׁה וּמַלְכוּת, בְּרָכוֹת וְהוֹדָאוֹת לְשִׁמְךָ הַגָּדוֹל וְהַקָּדוֹשׁ. וּמֵעוֹלָם וְעַד עוֹלָם אַתָּה אֵל: יְהַלְלוּךָ יְיָ אֱלֹהֵינוּ כָּל מַעֲשֶׂיךָ. וַחֲסִידֶיךָ צַדִּיקִים עוֹשֵׂי רְצוֹנֶךָ וְעַמְּךָ בֵּית יִשְׂרָאֵל כֻּלָּם בְּרִנָּה יוֹדוּ וִיבָרְכוּ וִישַׁבְּחוּ וִיפָאֲרוּ אֶת שֵׁם כְּבוֹדֶךָ. כִּי לְךָ טוֹב לְהוֹדוֹת וּלְשִׁמְךָ נָעִים לְזַמֵּר. וּמֵעוֹלָם וְעַד עוֹלָם אַתָּה אֵל: בָּרוּךְ אַתָּה יְיָ מֶלֶךְ מְהֻלָּל בַּתִּשְׁבָּחוֹת.

כוס רביעית
הנני מוכן ומזומן לקיים מצות כוס רביעי של ארבע כוסות לשם יחוד קדשא בריך הוא ושכינתיה, על ידי ההוא טמיר ונעלם בשם כל ישראל.

בָּרוּךְ אַתָּה יְיָ אֱלֹהֵינוּ מֶלֶךְ הָעוֹלָם בּוֹרֵא פְּרִי הַגָּפֶן.

שותים כוס רביעית בהסבת שמאל

בָּרוּךְ אַתָּה יְיָ אֱלֹהֵינוּ מֶלֶךְ הָעוֹלָם עַל הַגֶּפֶן וְעַל פְּרִי הַגֶּפֶן. וְעַל תְּנוּבַת הַשָּׂדֶה וְעַל אֶרֶץ חֶמְדָּה טוֹבָה וּרְחָבָה שֶׁרָצִיתָ וְהִנְחַלְתָּ לַאֲבוֹתֵינוּ לֶאֱכוֹל מִפִּרְיָהּ וְלִשְׂבּוֹעַ מִטּוּבָהּ. רַחֵם יְיָ אֱלֹהֵינוּ עָלֵינוּ וְעַל יִשְׂרָאֵל עַמֶּךָ, וְעַל יְרוּשָׁלַיִם עִירֶךָ, וְעַל צִיּוֹן מִשְׁכַּן כְּבוֹדֶךָ וְעַל מִזְבְּחֶךָ וְעַל הֵיכָלֶךָ. וּבְנֵה יְרוּשָׁלַיִם עִיר הַקֹּדֶשׁ בִּמְהֵרָה בְיָמֵינוּ. וְהַעֲלֵנוּ לְתוֹכָהּ. וְשַׂמְּחֵנוּ בְּבִנְיָנָהּ. וְנֹאכַל מִפִּרְיָהּ וְנִשְׂבַּע מִטּוּבָהּ. וּנְבָרֶכְךָ עָלֶיהָ בִּקְדֻשָּׁה וּבְטָהֳרָה. (בשבת אומרים: וּרְצֵה וְהַחֲלִיצֵנוּ בְּיוֹם הַשַּׁבָּת הַזֶּה) וְשַׂמְּחֵנוּ יְיָ אֱלֹהֵינוּ בְּיוֹם חַג הַמַּצּוֹת הַזֶּה. כִּי אַתָּה יְיָ טוֹב וּמֵטִיב לַכֹּל וְנוֹדֶה לְךָ עַל הָאָרֶץ וְעַל פְּרִי הַגָּפֶן:

בָּרוּךְ אַתָּה יְיָ עַל הָאָרֶץ וְעַל פְּרִי הַגָּפֶן:

So may Your name be praised for all eternity, our King, ruler who is great and holy in heaven and on the earth. To You, Lord our God, it is fitting to render song and praise, psalms of power and might, glory and honor, victory, beauty, holiness and sovereignty, blessings and thanks. Forever and ever You are God. All Your deeds are worthy of praise, Oh Lord. And the righteous followers, who do Your will, and all the house of Israel praise, thank, bless, glorify, extol, exalt, revere, sanctify, and adorn Your name, our King. It is fitting to give thanks unto You, and to sing praises to You, for You are God eternal. Blessed are You, Oh Lord, adored King, revered in praises. (Fourth cup of wine) Blessed are You, Oh Lord our God, who created the fruit of the vine. Blessed are you, Oh Lord our God, for the vine and the fruit of the vine And for the harvest of the field, and for the beautiful and spacious land You gave our fathers as an inheritance to eat of its fruits and enjoy its bounty. Have compassion, Lord our God, on Israel Your people, and on Jerusalem Your city, on Zion Your glorious abode, Your altar and Your Temple. Rebuild Jerusalem speedily, in our days. And bring us to it to rejoice in its restoration. Let us bless You in holiness and in purity. (On the Sabbath add: Grant us strength on the Sabbath day.) Make us rejoice, Oh Lord our God, on this holiday of the Matzot. For You are gracious and beneficient to all, and we thank You for our land and for the fruit of the vine. Blessed are You, Oh Lord our God, for the land and the fruit of its vineyards.

U'vechen yishtabach shimcha laad malkeinu, ha'el ha'melech hagadol ve'hakadosh bashamayim u'va'aretz, ki lecha naee Adonay Eloheinu, veilohei avoteinu le'olam va'ed. Shir u'shevacha, halel ve'zimra, oz u'memshala, netzach, gedula u'gevura, tehila ve'tif'eret, kedusha u'malchut, berachot ve'hodaot leshimcha ha'gadol ve'ha'kadosh. U'meolam ve'ad olam ata el:

Yehalelucha Adonay Eloheinu kol maasecha. Va'chasidecha tzadikim osei retzonecha ve'amcha beit Israel kulam berina yodu viyvarchu viyshabchu viyfaaru et shem kevodecha. Ki lecha tov lehodot, leshimcha naim lezamer. U'meolam ve'ad olam ata el: baruch ata Adonay melech mehulal batishbachot. Baruch ata Adonay, Eloheinu melech ha'olam, bore pri ha'gafen. Baruch ata, Adonay, Eloheinu melech ha'olam, al ha'gefen ve'al peri ha'gefen, ve'al tenuvat ha'sade, ve'al eretz chemda tova u'rechava, sheratzita ve'hinchalta la'avoteinu, le'echol mipirya ve'lisboa mituva. Rachem, Adonay Eloheinu, aleinu ve'al Israel amech, ve'al Yerushalayim ircha, ve'al Zion mishkan kevodach ve'al mizbechach ve'al heichalach. U'vne Yerushalaim ir hakodesh bimhera veyameinu. Ve'haalenu le'tocha, ve'samchenu bevinianah, ve'nochal mipirya, ve'nisba mituva. U'nevarechecha aleha bikducha uve'tohora. (Beshabat omrim: urtze ve'hachalitzenu beyom hashabat haze) ve'samchenu Adonay Eloheinu be'yom chag ha'matzot haze, ki ata, Adonay, tov u'meytiv lakol, ve'node lecha al ha'aretz ve'al peri ha'gafen:

BARUCH ATA ADONAY AL HA'ARETZ VE'AL PERI HA'GAFEN:

חֲסַל סִדּוּר פֶּסַח כְּהִלְכָתוֹ כְּכָל
מִשְׁפָּטוֹ וְחֻקָּתוֹ כַּאֲשֶׁר זָכִינוּ
לְסַדֵּר אוֹתוֹ כֵּן נִזְכֶּה לַעֲשׂוֹתוֹ.
זָךְ שׁוֹכֵן מְעוֹנָה קוֹמֵם
קְהַל עֲדַת מִי מָנָה בְּקָרוֹב נַהֵל
נִטְעֵי כַנָּה פְּדוּיִם לְצִיּוֹן בְּרִנָּה,
לְשָׁנָה הַבָּאָה
בִּירוּשָׁלָיִם הַבְּנוּיָה.

CONCLUSION OF THE SEDER

Now has our Seder been completed according to tradition, in all its rules and ordinances. As we have been privileged to hold this Seder tonight, so may we hold it again. May the Holy and Pure Lord on high make us an innumerable people again. May You soon redeem Israel, Your seed, and bring them joyously to Zion.

NEXT YEAR IN JERUSALEM!

NIRZAH

Chasal sidur pesach ke'hilchato ke'chol mishpato ve'chukato. Ka'asher zachinu lesader oto ken nizke la'asoto. Zach shochen meona komem kehal adat mi mana; be'karov nahel nit'ei Kana; peduyim lezion berina.
LESHANA HABAA BIYRUSHALAYIM HA'BENUYA!

בלילה הראשון של סדר פסח

אָז רֹב נִסִּים הִפְלֵאתָ בַּלַּיְלָה
בְּרֹאשׁ אַשְׁמוּרוֹת זֶה הַלַּיְלָה
גֵּר צֶדֶק נִצַּחְתּוֹ כְּנֶחֱלַק לוֹ לַיְלָה
וַיְהִי בַּחֲצִי הַלַּיְלָה

דַּנְתָּ מֶלֶךְ גְּרָר בַּחֲלוֹם הַלַּיְלָה
הִפְחַדְתָּ אֲרַמִּי בְּאֶמֶשׁ לַיְלָה
וַיִּשַּׂר יִשְׂרָאֵל לְמַלְאָךְ וַיּוּכַל לוֹ לַיְלָה
וַיְהִי בַּחֲצִי הַלַּיְלָה

זֶרַע בְּכוֹרֵי פַתְרוֹס מָחַצְתָּ בַּחֲצִי הַלַּיְלָה
חֵילָם לֹא מָצְאוּ בְּקוּמָם בַּלַּיְלָה
טִיסַת נְגִיד חֲרֹשֶׁת סִלִּיתָ בְכוֹכְבֵי לַיְלָה
וַיְהִי בַּחֲצִי הַלַּיְלָה

יָעַץ מְחָרֵף לְנוֹפֵף אִוּוּי הוֹבַשְׁתָּ פְּגָרָיו בַּלַּיְלָה
כָּרַע בֵּל וּמַצָּבוֹ בְּאִישׁוֹן לַיְלָה
לְאִישׁ חֲמוּדוֹת נִגְלָה רָז חֲזוֹת לַיְלָה
וַיְהִי בַּחֲצִי הַלַּיְלָה

מִשְׁתַּכֵּר בִּכְלֵי קֹדֶשׁ נֶהֱרַג בּוֹ בַּלַּיְלָה
נוֹשַׁע מִבּוֹר אֲרָיוֹת פּוֹתֵר בִּעֲתוּתֵי לַיְלָה
שִׂנְאָה נָטַר אֲגָגִי וְכָתַב סְפָרִים בַּלַּיְלָה
וַיְהִי בַּחֲצִי הַלַּיְלָה

עוֹרַרְתָּ נִצְחֲךָ עָלָיו בְּנֶדֶד שְׁנַת לַיְלָה
פּוּרָה תִדְרוֹךְ לְשׁוֹמֵר מַה מִלַּיְלָה
צָרַח כַּשּׁוֹמֵר וְשָׂח אָתָא בֹקֶר וְגַם לַיְלָה
וַיְהִי בַּחֲצִי הַלַּיְלָה

קָרֵב יוֹם אֲשֶׁר הוּא לֹא יוֹם וְלֹא לַיְלָה
רָם הוֹדַע כִּי לְךָ הַיּוֹם אַף לְךָ הַלַּיְלָה
שׁוֹמְרִים הַפְקֵד לְעִירְךָ כָּל הַיּוֹם וְכָל הַלַּיְלָה
תָּאִיר כְּאוֹר יוֹם חֶשְׁכַת לַיְלָה
וַיְהִי בַּחֲצִי הַלַּיְלָה

(On the first seder night, recite):
It happened at midnight. You performed many wonders that night, in the early sentry watches of the night. The righteous and sincere convert you caused to triumph at night. *It happened at midnight.*

You judged the King of Grar in a dream by night, and struck fear into the heart of the Aramite in the darkness. And Israel subdued an angel that night.
It happened at midnight.

And the seed, the firstborn of the Egyptians, You crushed that night. They had no strength when they arose at night. And Sisera, the prince of Haroshet, too, You defeated with the stars of the night.
It happened at midnight.

And the blasphemer You disgraced at night. And the idols fell in the darkness, and the dream was revealed to Daniel in the night. *It happened at midnight.*

And he who drank from the Temple's holy cup was killed at night. And Daniel was saved out of the lions' den and interpreted the visions of the night. And Haman, the evil Aggagite wrote his letters at night. *It happened at midnight.*

You triumphed then over the evil Haman on the king's sleepless night. Tread the winepress and answer those who ask about that night. The watchman shouts: morning follows the night.
It happened at midnight.

Bring quickly the day which is neither night nor day. Mighty Lord, set guards about Your city night and day. Make the darkness of the night as bright as day.
It happened at midnight.

Uvechen vayehi bachatzi halayla. Az rov nisim hifleta balayla. Berosh ashmurot ze halayla. Ger tzedek nitzachto kenechelak lo layla. Va'yehi bachatzi halayla. Danta melech Gerar bachalom halayla. Hifchadeta Arami be'emesh layla. Ve'Israel yasar la'el va'yuchal lo layla. Va'yehi bachatzi halayla. Zera bechorei Fatros machatzta bachatzi halayla. Cheylam lo matz'u vekumam balayla. Tisat negid Charoshet silita vekochvei layla. Va'yehi bachatzi halayla. Yaatz mecharef lenofef ivuy hovashta pegarav balayla. Kara bel u'matzavo be'ishon layla. Le'ish chamudot nigla raz chazot layla. Va'yehi bachatzi halayla. Mishtaker bichlei kodesh neherag bo balayla. Nosha' mibor arayot poter bi'atutei Layla. Sinaa natar Agagi ve'chatav sefarim balayla. Va'yehi bachatzi halayla. Orarta nitzchacha alav beneded shenat layla. Pura tidroch leshomer ma milayla. Tzarach kashomer ve'sach ata Boker ve'gam layla. Va'yehi bachatzi halayla. Karev yom asher hu lo yom ve'lo layla. Ram hoda' ki lecha hayom af lechah halayla. Shomerim hafked le'ircha kol hayom vechol ha'layla. Tair keor yom cheshkat layla. Va'yehi bachatzi halayla.

בלילה השני של סדר פסח

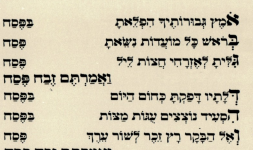

בְּפֶסַח	אֹמֶץ גְּבוּרוֹתֶיךָ הִפְלֵאתָ
פֶּסַח	בְּרֹאשׁ כָּל מוֹעֲדוֹת נִשֵּׂאתָ
פֶּסַח	גִּלִּיתָ לְאֶזְרָחִי חֲצוֹת לֵיל
וַאֲמַרְתֶּם זֶבַח פֶּסַח	
בְּפֶסַח	דְּלָתָיו דָּפַקְתָּ כְּחֹם הַיּוֹם
בְּפֶסַח	הִסְעִיד נוֹצְצִים עֻגוֹת מַצּוֹת
בְּפֶסַח	וְאֶל הַבָּקָר רָץ זֵכֶר לְשׁוֹר עֵרֶךְ
וַאֲמַרְתֶּם זֶבַח פֶּסַח	
בְּפֶסַח	זֹעֲמוּ סְדוֹמִים וְלֹהֲטוּ בָּאֵשׁ
פֶּסַח	חֻלַּץ לוֹט מֵהֶם וּמַצּוֹת אָפָה בְּקֵץ
בְּפֶסַח	טִאטֵאתָ אַדְמַת מֹף וְנֹף בְּעָבְרְךָ
וַאֲמַרְתֶּם זֶבַח פֶּסַח	
פֶּסַח	יָהּ, רֹאשׁ כָּל אוֹן מָחַצְתָּ בְּלֵיל שִׁמּוּר
פֶּסַח	כַּבִּיר עַל בֵּן בְּכוֹר פָּסַחְתָּ בְּדַם
בְּפֶסַח	לְבִלְתִּי תֵּת מַשְׁחִית לָבֹא בִּפְתָחַי
וַאֲמַרְתֶּם זֶבַח פֶּסַח	
פֶּסַח	מְסֻגֶּרֶת סֻגָּרָה בְּעִתּוֹתֵי
פֶּסַח	נִשְׁמְדָה מִדְיָן בִּצְלִיל שְׂעוֹרֵי עֹמֶר
פֶּסַח	שֹׂרְפוּ מִשְׁמַנֵּי פּוּל וְלוּד בִּיקַד יְקוֹד
וַאֲמַרְתֶּם זֶבַח פֶּסַח	
פֶּסַח	עוֹד הַיּוֹם בְּנֹב לַעֲמוֹד עַד גָּעָה עוֹנַת
בְּפֶסַח	פַּס יָד כָּתְבָה לְקַעֲקֵעַ צוּל
בְּפֶסַח	צָפֹה הַצָּפִית עָרוֹךְ הַשֻּׁלְחָן
וַאֲמַרְתֶּם זֶבַח פֶּסַח	
בְּפֶסַח	קָהָל כִּנְּסָה הֲדַסָּה צוֹם לְשַׁלֵּשׁ
בְּפֶסַח	רֹאשׁ מִבֵּית רָשָׁע מָחַצְתָּ בְּעֵץ חֲמִשִּׁים
בְּפֶסַח	שְׁתֵּי אֵלֶּה רֶגַע תָּבִיא לְעוּצִית
פֶּסַח	תָּעֹז יָדְךָ וְתָרוּם יְמִינְךָ כְּלֵיל הִתְקַדֵּשׁ חַג
וַאֲמַרְתֶּם זֶבַח פֶּסַח	

(On the night of the second Seder, recite):

AND YOU SHALL SAY:
IT IS THE PESACH SACRIFICE

You showed Your wondrous powers on Pesach
You made the most important feast on Pesach
You came to Abraham at midnight on Pesach
And you shall say: *It is the Pesach sacrifice*

You knocked at his door as if it were noon on Pesach
And he served the angels with Matzot on Pesach
He ran to bring the ox on Pesach
And you shall say: *It is the Pesach sacrifice*

The sinners of Sodom were burned on Pesach
Lot was saved to bake Matzot on Pesach
And You swept through Egypt and destroyed on Pesach
And you shall say: *It is the Pesach sacrifice*

Every Egyptian firstborn You crushed on Pesach
But Israel's firstborn You passed over on Pesach
So that no evil came to Israel on Pesach
And you shall say: *It is the Pesach sacrifice*

The fortified city fell on Pesach
Midian fell during the counting of the Omer from Pesach
Assyria's might was consumed in flame on Pesach
And you shall say: *It is the Pesach sacrifice*

Sennacherib would still be at Nov were it not for Pesach.
A hand sealed Babylon's fate on Pesach.
And its festive table was destroyed on Pesach.
And you shall say: *It is the Pesach sacrifice*

Esther called for a three-day fast on Pesach
And You hung the evil Haman on Pesach
Edom will be punished two-fold on Pesach
For Your mighty arm saves us on Pesach
And you shall say: *It is the Pesach sacrifice*

Uvechen ve'amartem zevach pesach. Ometz gevurotecha hifleta ba'pesach. Berosh kol mo'adot niseta pesach. Gilita le'ezrachi chatzot leil pesach. Va'amartem zevach pesach. Delatav dafakta kechom ha'yom bapesach. His'id notzetzim ugot matzot bapesach. Ve'el ha'bakar ratz zecher le'shor erech pesach. Va'amartem zevach pesach. Zoamu Sedomim ve'luhatu ve'esh bapesach. Chulatz Lot meihem u'matzot afa beketz pesach. Ti'teta admat mof ve'nof beovrecha bapesach. Va'amartem zevach pesach. Ya, rosh kol on machatzta beleil shimur pesach. Kabir al ben bechor pasachta bedam pesach. Levilti tet mashchit lavo bifetachai bapesach. Va'amartem zevach pesach. Mesugeret sugara be'itotei pesach. Nishmeda Midyan bitzlil seorei omer pesach. Sorfu mishmanei pul ve'lud biykad yekod pesach. Va'amartem zevach pesach. Od ha'yom benov laamod ad gaa onat pesach. Pas yad katva le'ka'ake'a tzul bapesach. Tzafo ha'tzafit aroch ha'shulchan bapesach. Va'amartem zevach pesach. Kahal kinsa Hadasa tzom leshalesh pesach. Rosh mibeit rasha machatzta be'etz chamishim bapesach. Shetei ele rega tavi le'utzit bapesach. Taoz yadcha ve'tarum yeminecha keleil hitkadesh chag pesach. Va'amartem zevach pesach.

אַדִּיר בִּמְלוּכָה	בָּחוּר כַּהֲלָכָה	גְּדוּדָיו יֹאמְרוּ לוֹ	לְךָ וּלְךָ, לְךָ כִּי לְךָ, לְךָ אַף לְךָ, לְךָ יְיָ הַמַּמְלָכָה. כִּי לוֹ נָאֶה, כִּי לוֹ יָאֶה:
דָּגוּל בִּמְלוּכָה	הָדוּר כַּהֲלָכָה	וָתִיקָיו יֹאמְרוּ לוֹ	לְךָ וּלְךָ, לְךָ כִּי לְךָ, לְךָ אַף לְךָ, לְךָ יְיָ הַמַּמְלָכָה. כִּי לוֹ נָאֶה, כִּי לוֹ יָאֶה:
זַכַּאי בִּמְלוּכָה	חָסִין כַּהֲלָכָה	טַפְסְרָיו יֹאמְרוּ לוֹ	לְךָ וּלְךָ, לְךָ כִּי לְךָ, לְךָ אַף לְךָ, לְךָ יְיָ הַמַּמְלָכָה. כִּי לוֹ נָאֶה, כִּי לוֹ יָאֶה:
יָחִיד בִּמְלוּכָה	כַּבִּיר כַּהֲלָכָה	לִמּוּדָיו יֹאמְרוּ לוֹ	לְךָ וּלְךָ, לְךָ כִּי לְךָ, לְךָ אַף לְךָ, לְךָ יְיָ הַמַּמְלָכָה. כִּי לוֹ נָאֶה, כִּי לוֹ יָאֶה:
מֶלֶךְ בִּמְלוּכָה	נוֹרָא כַּהֲלָכָה	סְבִיבָיו יֹאמְרוּ לוֹ	לְךָ וּלְךָ, לְךָ כִּי לְךָ, לְךָ אַף לְךָ, לְךָ יְיָ הַמַּמְלָכָה. כִּי לוֹ נָאֶה, כִּי לוֹ יָאֶה:
עָנָיו בִּמְלוּכָה	פּוֹדֶה כַּהֲלָכָה	צַדִּיקָיו יֹאמְרוּ לוֹ	לְךָ וּלְךָ, לְךָ כִּי לְךָ, לְךָ אַף לְךָ, לְךָ יְיָ הַמַּמְלָכָה. כִּי לוֹ נָאֶה, כִּי לוֹ יָאֶה:
קָדוֹשׁ בִּמְלוּכָה	רַחוּם כַּהֲלָכָה	שִׁנְאַנָּיו יֹאמְרוּ לוֹ	לְךָ וּלְךָ, לְךָ כִּי לְךָ, לְךָ אַף לְךָ, לְךָ יְיָ הַמַּמְלָכָה. כִּי לוֹ נָאֶה, כִּי לוֹ יָאֶה:
תַּקִּיף בִּמְלוּכָה	תּוֹמֵךְ כַּהֲלָכָה	תְּמִימָיו יֹאמְרוּ לוֹ	לְךָ וּלְךָ, לְךָ כִּי לְךָ, לְךָ אַף לְךָ, לְךָ יְיָ הַמַּמְלָכָה. כִּי לוֹ נָאֶה, כִּי לוֹ יָאֶה:

Beautiful praise befits the Lord

Mighty in His kingship, justly chosen. His followers sing: You, Oh Lord, You alone reign in Your majestic kingdom. Beautiful praise befits the Lord. He is known for His glorious rule: the faithful sing to Him: You, Oh Lord, You alone reign in Your majestic kingdom. Beautiful praise befits the Lord. Perfect in His kingship, justly strong, His angels sing to Him: You, Oh Lord, You alone reign in Your majestic kingdom. Beautiful praise befits the Lord. Alone He reigns, in righteous power, His scholars sing to Him: You, Oh Lord, You alone reign in Your majestic kingdom. Beautiful praise befits the Lord. He commands in His kingdom, revered by all, those near Him sing: You, Oh Lord, You alone reign in Your majestic kingdom. Beautiful praise befits the Lord. He is humble, and redeeming, and the righteous sing to Him: You, Oh Lord, You alone reign in Your majestic kingdom. Beautiful praise befits the Lord. Holy is He in kingship, and merciful, and His angels sing to Him: You, Oh Lord, You alone reign in Your majestic kingdom. Beautiful praise befits the Lord. He is strong and indomitable in His kingship, and the innocent sing unto Him: You, Oh Lord, You alone reign in Your majestic kingdom. Beautiful praise befits the Lord.

KI LO NA'EH KI LO YA'EH

Adir bimelucha, bachur kahalacha, gedudav yomru lo: lecha u'lecha, lecha ki lecha, lecha af lecha, lecha Adonay hamamlacha. Ki lo na'eh, ki lo ya'eh. Dagul bimelucha, hadur kahalacha, vatikav yomru lo: lecha u'lech, lecha ki lecha, lecha af lecha, lecha Adonay hamamlacha. Ki lo na'eh, ki lo ya'eh. Zakai bimelucha, chasin kahalacha, tafsarav yomru lo: lecha u'lecha, lecha ki lecha, lecha af lecha, lecha Adonay hamamlacha. Ki lo na'eh, ki lo ya'eh. Yachid bimelucha, kabir kahalacha, limudav yomru lo: lecha u'lecha, lecha ki lecha, lecha af lecha, lecha Adonay hamamlacha. Ki lo na'eh, ki lo ya'eh. Melech bimelucha, nora kahalacha, sevivav yomru lo: lecha u'lecha, lecha ki lecha, lecha af lecha, lecha Adonay hamamlacha. Ki lo na'eh, ki lo ya'eh. Anav bimelucha, podeh kahalacha, tzadikav yomru lo: lecha u'lecha, lecha ki lecha, lecha af lecha, lecha Adonay hamamlacha. Ki lo na'eh, ki lo ya'eh. Kadosh bimelucha, rachum kahalacha, shin'anav yomru lo: lecha u'lecha, lecha ki lecha, lecha af lecha, lecha Adonay hamamlacha. Ki lo na'eh, ki lo ya'eh. Takif bimelucha, tomech kahalacha, temimav yomru lo: lecha u'lecha, lecha ki lecha, lecha af lecha, lecha Adonay hamamlacha. KI LO NA'EH KI LO YA'EH.

יִבְנֶה בֵיתוֹ בְּקָרוֹב, בִּמְהֵרָה בִּמְהֵרָה, בְּיָמֵינוּ בְקָרוֹב. אֵל בְּנֵה, אֵל בְּנֵה, בְּנֵה בֵיתְךָ בְּקָרוֹב. בָּחוּר הוּא, גָּדוֹל הוּא, דָּגוּל הוּא,

יִבְנֶה בֵיתוֹ בְּקָרוֹב, בִּמְהֵרָה בִּמְהֵרָה, בְּיָמֵינוּ בְקָרוֹב. אֵל בְּנֵה, אֵל בְּנֵה, בְּנֵה בֵיתְךָ בְּקָרוֹב. הָדוּר הוּא, וָתִיק הוּא, חָסִיד הוּא,

יִבְנֶה בֵיתוֹ בְּקָרוֹב, בִּמְהֵרָה בִּמְהֵרָה, בְּיָמֵינוּ בְקָרוֹב. אֵל בְּנֵה, אֵל בְּנֵה, בְּנֵה בֵיתְךָ בְּקָרוֹב. טָהוֹר הוּא, יָחִיד הוּא, כַּבִּיר הוּא, לָמוּד הוּא, מֶלֶךְ הוּא, נוֹרָא הוּא, סַגִּיב הוּא, עִזּוּז הוּא, פּוֹדֶה הוּא, צַדִּיק הוּא,

יִבְנֶה בֵיתוֹ בְּקָרוֹב, בִּמְהֵרָה בִּמְהֵרָה, בְּיָמֵינוּ בְקָרוֹב. אֵל בְּנֵה, אֵל בְּנֵה, בְּנֵה בֵיתְךָ בְּקָרוֹב. קָדוֹשׁ הוּא, רַחוּם הוּא, שַׁדַּי הוּא, תַּקִּיף הוּא,

יִבְנֶה בֵיתוֹ בְּקָרוֹב, בִּמְהֵרָה בִּמְהֵרָה, בְּיָמֵינוּ בְקָרוֹב. אֵל בְּנֵה, אֵל בְּנֵה, בְּנֵה בֵיתְךָ בְּקָרוֹב:

Awesome is the Lord's power

May He re-build His temple in our day. Brave is He, Colossal and Divine in His splendor. May He re-build His temple in our day. Excellent is He, without Fault, His Greatness is due all Honor. May He re-build His temple in our day. Immortal is the Lord, Just, His Knowledge is Lustrous, He is Master of the Universe. No force can equal His. Over all the earth His reign is Perfect, the Quintessence of Righteousness. May He re-build His temple in our day. Sagacious beyond compare. Tender to those in need, Understanding to the lost and wayward. The Lord is Vibrant and He is Wonderful. He is the Lord. May He re-build His temple in our day.

Adir hu,

yivneh veito bekarov, bimhera bimhera, be'yameinu ve'karov. El bene, el bene, bene veitcha bekarov. Bachur hu, gadol hu, dagul hu, yivne veito bekarov... Hadur hu, vatick hu, chasid hu, yivne veito bekarov... Tahor hu, yachid hu, kabir hu, lamud hu, melech hu, nora hu, sagiv hu, izuz hu, podeh hu, tzadik hu, yivne veito bekarov... Kadosh hu, rachum hu, shaday hu, takif hu, yivne veito bekarov, bimhera bimhera, be'yameinu bekarov. El bene, el bene, bene veitcha bekarov.

Who knows one?
I know one,
One is our God
in heaven and on earth

Who knows two?
I know two. Two are the tablets
of the Covenant One is our God
in heaven and on earth.

Who knows three?
I know three. Three are the
Patriarchs. Two are the tablets of
the Covenant. One is our God in
heaven and on earth.

Who knows four?
I know four. Four are the
Matriarchs. Three are the Patriarchs.
Two are the tablets of the
Covenant. One is our God in
heaven and on earth.

Who knows five?
I know five. Five are the books
of the Torah. Four are the
Matriarchs. Three are the
Patriarchs. Two are the tablets of
the Covenant. One is our God in
heaven and on earth.

מִי יוֹדֵעַ
אֶחָד אֲנִי יוֹדֵעַ
אֶחָד אֱלֹהֵינוּ שֶׁבַּשָּׁמַיִם וּבָאָרֶץ

שְׁנַיִם מִי יוֹדֵעַ
שְׁנַיִם אֲנִי יוֹדֵעַ,
שְׁנֵי לוּחוֹת הַבְּרִית,
אֶחָד אֱלֹהֵינוּ שֶׁבַּשָּׁמַיִם וּבָאָרֶץ

שְׁלוֹשָׁה מִי יוֹדֵעַ
שְׁלוֹשָׁה אֲנִי יוֹדֵעַ,
שְׁלוֹשָׁה אָבוֹת,
שְׁנֵי לוּחוֹת הַבְּרִית,
אֶחָד אֱלֹהֵינוּ שֶׁבַּשָּׁמַיִם וּבָאָרֶץ

אַרְבַּע מִי יוֹדֵעַ
אַרְבַּע אֲנִי יוֹדֵעַ,
אַרְבַּע אִמָּהוֹת, שְׁלוֹשָׁה אָבוֹת,
שְׁנֵי לוּחוֹת הַבְּרִית,
אֶחָד אֱלֹהֵינוּ שֶׁבַּשָּׁמַיִם וּבָאָרֶץ

חֲמִשָּׁה מִי יוֹדֵעַ
חֲמִשָּׁה אֲנִי יוֹדֵעַ,
חֲמִשָּׁה חֻמְשֵׁי תוֹרָה,
אַרְבַּע אִמָּהוֹת, שְׁלוֹשָׁה אָבוֹת,
שְׁנֵי לוּחוֹת הַבְּרִית,
אֶחָד אֱלֹהֵינוּ שֶׁבַּשָּׁמַיִם וּבָאָרֶץ

Echad mi yodea?
Echad ani yodea:
Echad eloheinu
shebashamayim
u'va'aretz.

Shenayim mi yodea?
Shenayim ani yodea:
shenei luchot ha'berit,
echad eloheinu
shebashamayim
u'va'aretz.

Shelosha mi yodea?
Shelosha ani yodea:
shelosha avot, shenei
luchot ba'berit, echad
eloheinu
shebashamayim
u'va'aretz.

Arba mi yodea?
Arba ani yodea: arba
imahot, shelosha avot,
shenei luchot ba'berit,
echad eloheinu
shebashamayim
u'va'aretz.

Chamisha mi yodea?
Chamisha ani yodea:
chamisha chumshei
torah, arba imahot,
shelosha avot, shenei
luchot ba'berit, echad
eloheinu shebashamayim
u'va'aretz.

Who knows six?
I know six. Six are the sections of the Mishnah. Five are the books of the Torah. Four are the Matriarchs. Three are the Patriarchs. Two are the tablets of the Covenant. One is our God in heaven and on earth.

Who knows seven?
I know seven. Seven are the days of the week. Six are the sections of the Mishnah. Five are the books of the Torah. Four are the Matriarchs. Three are the Patriarchs. Two are the tablets of the Covenant. One is our God in heaven and on earth.

Who knows eight?
I know eight. Eight are the days before circumcision. Seven are the days of the week. Six are the sections of the Mishnah. Five are the books of the Torah. Four are the Matriarchs. Three are the Patriarchs. Two are the tablets of the Covenant. One is our God in heaven and on earth.

Who knows nine?
I know nine. Nine are the months of child-bearing. Eight are the days before circumcision. Seven are the days of the week. Six are the sections of the Mishnah. Five are the books of the Torah. Four are the Matriarchs. Three are the Patriarchs. Two are the tablets of the Covenant. One is our God in heaven and on earth.

Who knows ten?
I know ten. There are ten commandments. Nine are the months of child-bearing. Eight are the days before circumcision. Seven are the days of the week. Six are the sections of the Mishnah. Five are the books of the Torah. Four are the Matriarchs. Three are the Patriarchs. Two are the tablets of the Covenant. One is our God in heaven on on earth.

שִׁשָּׁה מִי יוֹדֵעַ,
שִׁשָּׁה אֲנִי יוֹדֵעַ,
שִׁשָּׁה סִדְרֵי מִשְׁנָה, חֲמִשָּׁה חֻמְשֵׁי תוֹרָה,
אַרְבַּע אִמָּהוֹת, שְׁלוֹשָׁה אָבוֹת,
שְׁנֵי לוּחוֹת הַבְּרִית,
אֶחָד אֱלֹהֵינוּ שֶׁבַּשָּׁמַיִם וּבָאָרֶץ

שִׁבְעָה מִי יוֹדֵעַ,
שִׁבְעָה אֲנִי יוֹדֵעַ,
שִׁבְעָה יְמֵי שַׁבַּתָּא,
שִׁשָּׁה סִדְרֵי מִשְׁנָה, חֲמִשָּׁה חֻמְשֵׁי תוֹרָה,
אַרְבַּע אִמָּהוֹת, שְׁלוֹשָׁה אָבוֹת,
שְׁנֵי לוּחוֹת הַבְּרִית,
אֶחָד אֱלֹהֵינוּ שֶׁבַּשָּׁמַיִם וּבָאָרֶץ

שְׁמוֹנָה מִי יוֹדֵעַ,
שְׁמוֹנָה אֲנִי יוֹדֵעַ,
שְׁמוֹנָה יְמֵי מִילָה,
שִׁבְעָה יְמֵי שַׁבַּתָּא,
שִׁשָּׁה סִדְרֵי מִשְׁנָה, חֲמִשָּׁה חֻמְשֵׁי תוֹרָה,
אַרְבַּע אִמָּהוֹת, שְׁלוֹשָׁה אָבוֹת,
שְׁנֵי לוּחוֹת הַבְּרִית,
אֶחָד אֱלֹהֵינוּ שֶׁבַּשָּׁמַיִם וּבָאָרֶץ

תִּשְׁעָה מִי יוֹדֵעַ,
תִּשְׁעָה אֲנִי יוֹדֵעַ,
תִּשְׁעָה יַרְחֵי לֵדָה,
שְׁמוֹנָה יְמֵי מִילָה, שִׁבְעָה יְמֵי שַׁבַּתָּא,
שִׁשָּׁה סִדְרֵי מִשְׁנָה, חֲמִשָּׁה חֻמְשֵׁי תוֹרָה,
אַרְבַּע אִמָּהוֹת, שְׁלוֹשָׁה אָבוֹת,
שְׁנֵי לוּחוֹת הַבְּרִית,
אֶחָד אֱלֹהֵינוּ שֶׁבַּשָּׁמַיִם וּבָאָרֶץ.

עֲשָׂרָה מִי יוֹדֵעַ,
עֲשָׂרָה אֲנִי יוֹדֵעַ,
עֲשָׂרָה דִבְּרַיָּא,
תִּשְׁעָה יַרְחֵי לֵדָה, שְׁמוֹנָה יְמֵי מִילָה,
שִׁבְעָה יְמֵי שַׁבַּתָּא,
שִׁשָּׁה סִדְרֵי מִשְׁנָה, חֲמִשָּׁה חֻמְשֵׁי תוֹרָה,
אַרְבַּע אִמָּהוֹת, שְׁלוֹשָׁה אָבוֹת,
שְׁנֵי לוּחוֹת הַבְּרִית,
אֶחָד אֱלֹהֵינוּ שֶׁבַּשָּׁמַיִם וּבָאָרֶץ.

Shisha mi yodea? Shisha ani yodea: Shisha sidrei mishna, chamisha chumshei torah, arba imahaot, shelosha avot, shenei luchot ha'berit, echad Eloheinu shebashamayim u'va'aretz.

Shiv'a mi yodea? Shiv'a ani yodea: shiv'a yemei shabata, shisha sidrei mishna, chamisha chumshei torah, arba imahaot, shelosha avot, shenei luchot ha'berit, echad Eloheinu shebashamayim u'va'aretz.

Shemona mi yodea? Shemona ani yodea: shemona yemei mila, shiv'a yemei shabata, shisha sidrei mishna, chamisha chumshei torah, arba imahaot, shelosha avot, shenei luchot ha'berit, echad Eloheinu shebashamayim u'va'aretz.

Tish'a mi yodea? Tish'a ani yodea: tish'a yarchei leida, shemona yemei mila, shiv'a yemei shabata, shisha sidrei mishna, chamisha chumshei torah, arba imahaot, shelosha avot, shenei luchot ha'berit, echad Eloheinu shebashamayim u'va'aretz.

Asara mi yodea? Asara ani yodea: asara dibraya, tish'a yarchei leida, shemona yemei mila, shiv'a yemei shabata, shisha sidrei mishna, chamisha chumshei torah, arba imahaot, shelosha avot, shenei luchot ha'berit, echad Eloheinu shebashamayim u'va'aretz.

Who knows eleven?
I know Eleven. Eleven are the stars. Ten are the commandments. Nine are the months of child-bearing. Eight are the days before circumcision. Seven are the days of the week. Six are the sections of the Mishnah. Five are the books of the Torah. Four are the Matriarchs. Three are the Patriarchs. Two are the tablets of the Covenant. One is our God in heaven on on earth.

Who knows twelve?
I know twelve. Twelve are the tribes. Eleven are the stars. Ten are the commandments. Nine are the months of child-bearing. Eight are the days before circumcision. Seven are the days of the week. Six are the sections of the Mishnah. Five are the books of the Torah. Four are the Matriarchs. Three are the Patriarchs. Two are the tablets of the Covenant. One is our God in heaven on on earth.

Who knows thirteen?
I know thirteen. Thirteen are God's attributes. Twelve are the tribes. Eleven are the stars. Ten are the commandments. Nine are the months of child-bearing. Eight are the days before circumcision. Seven are the days of the week. Six are the sections of the Mishnah. Five are the books of the Torah. Four are the Matriarchs. Three are the Patriarchs. Two are the tablets of the Covenant. **One is our God in heaven on on earth.**

אַחַד עָשָׂר מִי יוֹדֵעַ
אַחַד עָשָׂר אֲנִי יוֹדֵעַ,
אַחַד עָשָׂר כּוֹכְבַיָּא,
עֲשָׂרָה דִבְּרַיָּא, תִּשְׁעָה יַרְחֵי לֵדָה,
שְׁמוֹנָה יְמֵי מִילָה, שִׁבְעָה יְמֵי שַׁבַּתָּא,
שִׁשָּׁה סִדְרֵי מִשְׁנָה, חֲמִשָּׁה חֻמְשֵׁי תוֹרָה,
אַרְבַּע אִמָּהוֹת, שְׁלוֹשָׁה אָבוֹת,
שְׁנֵי לוּחוֹת הַבְּרִית
אֶחָד אֱלֹהֵינוּ שֶׁבַּשָּׁמַיִם וּבָאָרֶץ

שְׁנֵים עָשָׂר מִי יוֹדֵעַ
שְׁנֵים עָשָׂר אֲנִי יוֹדֵעַ
שְׁנֵים עָשָׂר שִׁבְטַיָּא, אַחַד עָשָׂר כּוֹכְבַיָּא,
עֲשָׂרָה דִבְּרַיָּא תִּשְׁעָה יַרְחֵי לֵדָה
שְׁמוֹנָה יְמֵי מִילָה שִׁבְעָה יְמֵי שַׁבַּתָּא
שִׁשָּׁה סִדְרֵי מִשְׁנָה חֲמִשָּׁה חֻמְשֵׁי תוֹרָה
אַרְבַּע אִמָּהוֹת שְׁלוֹשָׁה אָבוֹת
שְׁנֵי לוּחוֹת הַבְּרִית
אֶחָד אֱלֹהֵינוּ שֶׁבַּשָּׁמַיִם וּבָאָרֶץ

שְׁלוֹשָׁה עָשָׂר מִי יוֹדֵעַ
שְׁלוֹשָׁה עָשָׂר אֲנִי יוֹדֵעַ
שְׁלוֹשָׁה עָשָׂר מִדַּיָּא
שְׁנֵים עָשָׂר שִׁבְטַיָּא אַחַד עָשָׂר כּוֹכְבַיָּא
עֲשָׂרָה דִבְּרַיָּא תִּשְׁעָה יַרְחֵי לֵדָה
שְׁמוֹנָה יְמֵי מִילָה שִׁבְעָה יְמֵי שַׁבַּתָּא
שִׁשָּׁה סִדְרֵי מִשְׁנָה חֲמִשָּׁה חֻמְשֵׁי תוֹרָה
אַרְבַּע אִמָּהוֹת שְׁלוֹשָׁה אָבוֹת
שְׁנֵי לוּחוֹת הַבְּרִית

Achad-asar mi yodea?
Achad-asar ani yodea: achad-asar kochvaya, asara dibraya, tish'a yarchei leida, shemona yemei mila, shiv'a yemei shabata, shisha sidrei mishna, chamisha chumshei torah, arba imahot, shelosha avot, shenei luchot ha'berit, echad eloheinu shebashamayim u'va'aretz.

Shneim-asar mi yodea?
Shneim-asar ani yodea: shneim-asar shivtaya, achad-asar kochvaya, asara dibraya, tish'a yarchei leida, shemona yemei mila, shiv'a yemei shabata, shisha sidrei mishna, chamisha chumshei torah, arba imahot, shelosha avot, shenei luchot ha'berit, echad eloheinu shebashamayim u'va'aretz.

Shlosha-asar mi yodea?
Shlosha-asar ani yodea: shlosha-asar midaya, shneim-asar shivtaya, achad-asar kochvaya, asara dibraya, tish'a yarchei leida, shemona yemei mila, shiv'a yemei shabata, shisha sidrei mishna, chamisha chumshei torah, arba imahot, shelosha avot, shenei luchot ha'berit, echad eloheinu shebashamayim u'va'aretz.

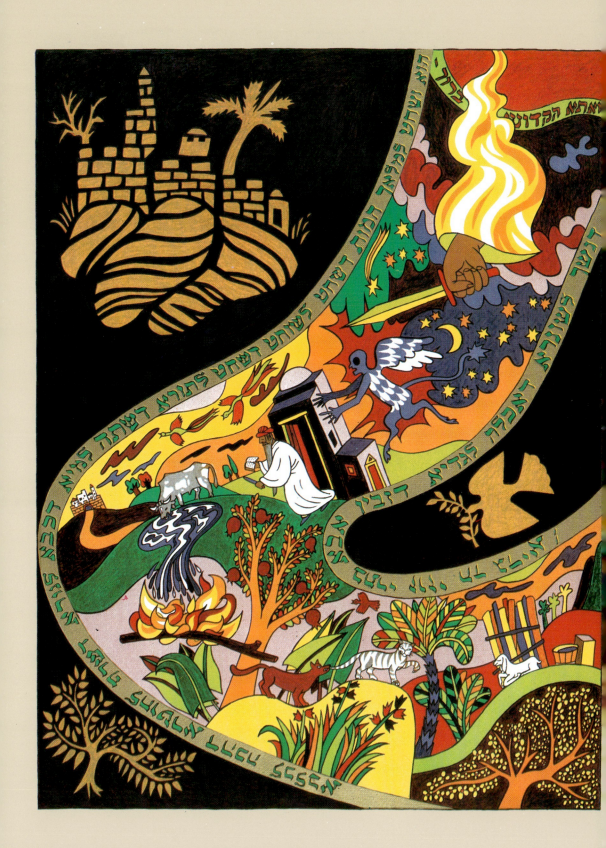

חַד גַּדְיָא

חַד גַּדְיָא, דְּזַבִּין אַבָּא בִּתְרֵי זוּזֵי חַד גַּדְיָא חַד גַּדְיָא.

וְאָתָא שׁוּנְרָא, וְאָכְלָה לְגַדְיָא, דְּזַבִּין אַבָּא בִּתְרֵי זוּזֵי, חַד גַּדְיָא חַד גַּדְיָא.

וְאָתָא כַלְבָּא, וְנָשַׁךְ לְשׁוּנְרָא, דְּאָכְלָה לְגַדְיָא,
דְּזַבִּין אַבָּא בִּתְרֵי זוּזֵי, חַד גַּדְיָא חַד גַּדְיָא.

וְאָתָא חוּטְרָא וְהִכָּה לְכַלְבָּא, דְּנָשַׁךְ לְשׁוּנְרָא, דְּאָכְלָה לְגַדְיָא,
דְּזַבִּין אַבָּא בִּתְרֵי זוּזֵי, חַד גַּדְיָא חַד גַּדְיָא.

וְאָתָא נוּרָא וְשָׂרַף לְחוּטְרָא, דְּהִכָּה לְכַלְבָּא, דְּנָשַׁךְ לְשׁוּנְרָא,
דְּאָכְלָה לְגַדְיָא, דְּזַבִּין אַבָּא בִּתְרֵי זוּזֵי, חַד גַּדְיָא חַד גַּדְיָא.

וְאָתָא מַיָּא וְכָבָה לְנוּרָא, דְּשָׂרַף לְחוּטְרָא, דְּהִכָּה לְכַלְבָּא,
דְּנָשַׁךְ לְשׁוּנְרָא, דְּאָכְלָה לְגַדְיָא,
דְּזַבִּין אַבָּא בִּתְרֵי זוּזֵי, חַד גַּדְיָא חַד גַּדְיָא.

וְאָתָא תוֹרָא וְשָׁתָה לְמַיָּא, דְּכָבָה לְנוּרָא, דְּשָׂרַף לְחוּטְרָא,
דְּהִכָּה לְכַלְבָּא, דְּנָשַׁךְ לְשׁוּנְרָא, דְּאָכְלָה לְגַדְיָא,
דְּזַבִּין אַבָּא בִּתְרֵי זוּזֵי, חַד גַּדְיָא חַד גַּדְיָא.

וְאָתָא הַשּׁוֹחֵט וְשָׁחַט לְתוֹרָא, דְּשָׁתָה לְמַיָּא, דְּכָבָה לְנוּרָא,
דְּשָׂרַף לְחוּטְרָא, דְּהִכָּה לְכַלְבָּא, דְּנָשַׁךְ לְשׁוּנְרָא,
דְּאָכְלָה לְגַדְיָא, דְּזַבִּין אַבָּא בִּתְרֵי זוּזֵי, חַד גַּדְיָא חַד גַּדְיָא.

וְאָתָא מַלְאַךְ הַמָּוֶת, וְשָׁחַט לְשׁוֹחֵט, דְּשָׁחַט לְתוֹרָא,
דְּשָׁתָה לְמַיָּא, דְּכָבָה לְנוּרָא, דְּשָׂרַף לְחוּטְרָא,
דְּהִכָּה לְכַלְבָּא, דְּנָשַׁךְ לְשׁוּנְרָא, דְּאָכְלָה לְגַדְיָא,
דְּזַבִּין אַבָּא בִּתְרֵי זוּזֵי, חַד גַּדְיָא חַד גַּדְיָא.

וְאָתָא הַקָּדוֹשׁ בָּרוּךְ הוּא, וְשָׁחַט לְמַלְאַךְ הַמָּוֶת,
דְּשָׁחַט לְשׁוֹחֵט, דְּשָׁחַט לְתוֹרָא, דְּשָׁתָה לְמַיָּא,
דְּכָבָה לְנוּרָא, דְּשָׂרַף לְחוּטְרָא, דְּהִכָּה לְכַלְבָּא,
דְּנָשַׁךְ לְשׁוּנְרָא, דְּאָכְלָה לְגַדְיָא,
דְּזַבִּין אַבָּא בִּתְרֵי זוּזֵי, חַד גַּדְיָא חַד גַּדְיָא.

HAD-GADYA Only One Kid

Only one kid, only one kid,
which my father bought for two zuzim. Only one kid, Only one kid.

Then came the cat and ate the kid
which my father bought for two zuzim. Only one kid, Only one kid.

Then came the dog and bit the cat which ate the kid
which myfather bought for two zuzim. Only one kid, Only one kid.

Then came the stick and hit the dog which bit the cat which ate the kid
which my father bought for two zuzim. Only one kid, Only one kid.

Then came the fire and burned the stick which hit the dog which bit the cat which ate the kid
which my father bought for two zuzim. Only one kid, Only one kid.

Then came the water and quenched the fire which burned the stick which hit the dog which
bit the cat which ate the kid which my father bought for two zuzim. Only one kid, Only kid.

Then came the ox and drank the water which quenched the fire which burned the stick
which hit the dog which bit the cat which ate the kid
which my father bought for two zuzim. Only one kid, Only one kid.

Then came the slaughterer and slaughtered the ox which drank the water which quenched
the fire which burned the stick which hit the dog which bit the cat which ate the kid
which my father bought for two zuzim. Only one kid, Only one kid.

Then came the angel of death and slew the slaughterer who killed the ox which drank the
water which quenched the fire which burned the stick which hit the dog which bit the cat
which ate the kid which my father bought for two zuzim. Only one kid, Only one kid.

Then came the Holy One Blessed be He and slew the Angel of Death who killed the
slaughterer who killed the ox which drank the water which quenched the fire which burned
the stick which hit the dog which bit the cat which ate the kid
which my father bought for two zuzim. Only one kid, Only one kid.

Chad Gadya

Chad Gadya, Dezabin aba bitrei zuzei, chad gadya, chad gadya.
Ve'ata shunra, ve'achla le'gadya, Dezabin aba bitrei zuzei chad gadya, chad gadya.
Ve'ata kalba, ve'nashach le'shunra, de'achla le'gadya,
Dezabin aba bitrei zuzei chad gadya, chad gadya.
Ve'ata chutra ve'hika le'chalba, de'nashach le'shunra, de'achla le'gadya.
Dezabin aba bitrei zuzei chad gadya, chad gadya.
Ve'ata nura, ve'saraf le'chutra, de'hika le'chalba, de'nashach le'shunra, de'achla le'gadya,
Dezabin aba bitrei zuzei, chad gadya, chad gadya.
Ve'ata maya ve'kava le'nura, de'saraf le'chutra, de'hika le'chalba, de'nashach
le'shunra, de'achla le'gadya,
Dezabin aba bitrei zuzei chad gadya, chad gadya.
Ve'ata tora, ve'shata le'maya, de'kava le'nura, de'saraf le'chutra,
de'hika le'chalba, de'nashach le'shunra, de'achla le'gadya,
Dezabin aba bitrei zuzei chad gadya, chad gadya.
Ve'ata ha'shochet ve'shachat le'tora, de'shata le'maya, de'kava le'nura, de'saraf
le'chutra, de'hika le'chalba, de'nashach leshunra, de'achla le'gadya,
Dezabin ata bitrei zuzei chad gadya, chad gadya.
Ve'ata malach ha'mavet, ve'shachat le'shochet, de'shachat le'tora, de'shata le'maya
de'kava le'nura, de'saraf le'chutra, de'hika le'chalba, de'nashach le'shunra, de'achla le'gadya,
Dezabin aba bitrei zuzei chad gadya, chad gadya.
Ve'ata ha'Kadosh Baruch Hu, ve'shachat le'malach ha'mavet, de'shachat
le'shochet, de'shachat le'tora, de'shata le'maya, de'kava le'nura de'saraf le'chutra,
de'hika le'chalba, de'nashach le'shunra, de'achla le'gadya,
Dezabin aba bitrei zuzei, chad gadya, chad gadya.

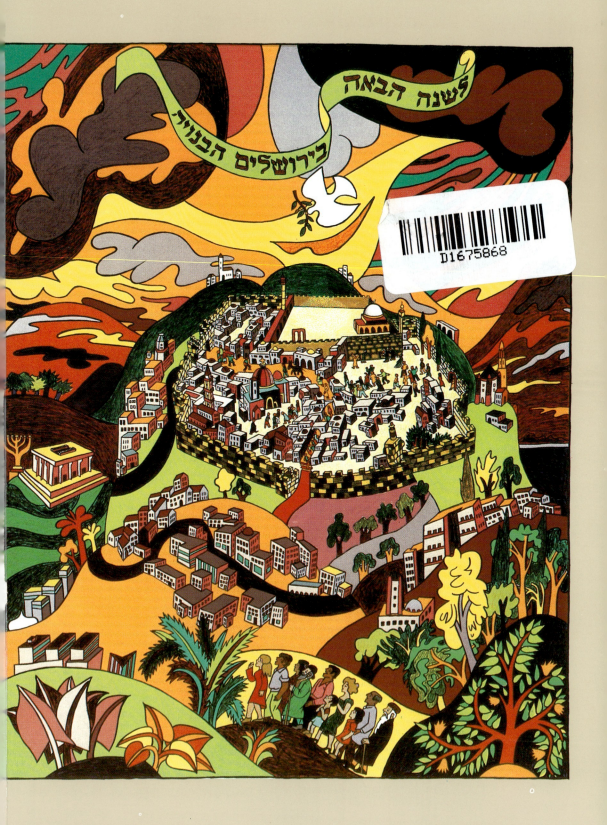